The Math Coach Field Guide

The Math Coach Field Guide

Charting Your Course

EDITED BY

CAROLYN FELUX *and* PAULA SNOWDY

FOREWORD BY

MARILYN BURNS

MATH SOLUTIONS PUBLICATIONS
SAUSALITO, CA

Math Solutions Publications
A division of
Marilyn Burns Education Associates
150 Gate 5 Road, Suite 101
Sausalito, CA 94965
www.mathsolutions.com

Copyright © 2006 by Math Solutions Publications

Library of Congress Cataloging-in-Publication Data

The math coach field guide : charting your course / edited by Carolyn Felux and Paula Snowdy ; foreword by Marilyn Burns.
p. cm.
Includes bibliographical references.
ISBN-13: 978-0-941355-72-8 (acid-free paper)
ISBN-10: 0-941355-72-1 (acid-free paper)
1. Mathematics—Study and teaching (Elementary) 2. Mathematics—Study and teaching (Middle school) I. Felux, Carolyn. II. Snowdy, Paula.
QA11.2.M268 2006
510.71—dc22

2006017077

EDITOR: Toby Gordon
PRODUCTION: Melissa L. Inglis
COVER DESIGN: Isaac Tobin
INTERIOR DESIGN: Jenny Jensen Greenleaf
COMPOSITION: Interactive Composition Corporation

Printed in the United States of America on acid-free paper
10 09 08 07   ML   3 4 5

A Message from Marilyn Burns

We at Math Solutions Professional Development believe that teaching math well calls for increasing our understanding of the math we teach, seeking deeper insights into how children learn mathematics, and refining our lessons to best promote students' learning.

Math Solutions Publications shares classroom-tested lessons and teaching expertise from our faculty of Math Solutions Inservice instructors as well as from other respected math educators. Our publications are part of the nationwide effort we've made since 1984 that now includes

- more than five hundred face-to-face inservice programs each year for teachers and administrators in districts across the country;
- annually publishing professional development books, now totaling more than sixty titles and spanning the teaching of all math topics in kindergarten through grade 8;
- four series of videotapes for teachers, plus a videotape for parents, that show math lessons taught in actual classrooms;
- on-site visits to schools to help refine teaching strategies and assess student learning; and
- free online support, including grade-level lessons, book reviews, inservice information, and district feedback, all in our quarterly *Math Solutions Online Newsletter.*

For information about all of the products and services we have available, please visit our website at *www.mathsolutions.com.* You can also contact us to discuss math professional development needs by calling (800) 868-9092 or by sending an email to *info@mathsolutions.com.*

We're always eager for your feedback and interested in learning about your particular needs. We look forward to hearing from you.

Math Solutions.
PUBLICATIONS

Contents

Foreword

BY MARILYN BURNS

Some of my colleagues are currently math coaches. Actually, they aren't all called math coaches. Different titles exist for this position—math coach, math specialist, math support teacher, math resource teacher, and more. And just as there isn't consistency with my colleagues' titles, there isn't much consistency with their responsibilities. Some have district positions and are responsible for serving teachers in several schools; others are assigned to one particular school. Some provide support to classroom teachers with whom they previously taught, now faced with the sometimes delicate task of carving out new forms of relationships; others have positions in schools new to them, now faced with building new collaborative relationships that are based on trust and respect. Also, the schools they serve have different approaches to teaching math, use different instructional programs, have different materials available, and have school administrators with different styles.

With all of the variations and differences, a common goal guides math coaches—to support the mathematics learning of all students by supporting teachers to improve their teaching of mathematics. The question of how to provide math coaches the support they need to meet this goal was the spark for this book. What makes a coach effective? What is important for a coach to think about in the role of supporting other teachers? What successes have other coaches experienced? What pitfalls have others encountered, and what have they done about them?

This book was conceived to help math coaches learn from one another. Each coach who contributed to the book has firsthand experience as a math coach and has grappled with a range of challenges and issues. With the same spirit that helped them dig into their first coaching position, these experts agreed to contribute a chapter to this book by looking at their work, identifying a focus, and digging into writing. By doing this, they again stepped into new waters, shifting from helping classroom teachers to communicating with other coaches.

We struggled over the title of the book for quite a while and brainstormed a long list before settling on *The Math Coach Field Guide: Charting Your Course*. This title felt especially right to me as a beginning birder. I have a number of field guides about birds, all with different approaches and different formats. Some are guides that I like to have at hand when I'm out in the field or on the back deck, while others I keep on the shelf and reach for when I'm searching for a particular piece of information. Some focus on a smaller region, while others provide a broader look. But with all the differences, what's the same about them is that the authors all love birds and are interested in communicating their knowledge and enthusiasm.

In that spirit, the chapters in this field guide were all written by teachers who love teaching and are interested in communicating their knowledge and enthusiasm for the role they've taken on as a math coach. In a way, it would be wonderful to have a field guide from each of them. While that's a dream to hold, I know that most coaches are working way too hard to have time for writing an entire book. Right now, I'm appreciative that they took on the challenge of contributing to this book, which was in itself a huge effort.

This book isn't meant to be read cover to cover. Rather, it's a book for you to dip in and out of, depending on your particular need. However, I do suggest that you begin with the introduction by the book's editors, Carolyn Felux and Paula Snowdy. Carolyn and Paula are both master teachers, experienced coaches, and Math Solutions Education Specialists. Each has a great deal of experience coaching coaches. Their introduction provides thumbnail descriptions of the chapters and offers a guide to help you select your own starting place.

Introduction

BY CAROLYN FELUX AND PAULA SNOWDY

I remember well the day when I hesitantly agreed to become a math coach in my school, fourteen years ago. Supporting teachers and a principal on a journey to creating quality programs where children truly understood mathematics was a goal that seemed daunting to me. I felt unsure of my own abilities to do and teach mathematics, so how could I help others? It was clearly an enormous, complex task and I didn't know where to begin.

—CHRIS CONFER

In recent years, a growing number of math coaches and specialists across the country have been designated to help teachers and schools improve mathematics instruction. And like Chris, many begin this new role with a title and a charge—but seldom a road map. *The Math Coach Field Guide: Charting Your Course* is not a road map; the roles and responsibilities of math coaches and specialists are far too complex for that. It is, however, a resource compiled for coaches by coaches. In the book's eleven chapters, math coaches provide glimpses into their challenges, false starts, and successes in supporting and improving math instruction in their schools. While the accounts convey the passion, persistence, and vision that successful coaches bring to their work, they also provide windows into the details and strategies.

Some of the authors take a broad approach that identifies the landscape of the coach's role. For example, in the book's opening chapter, math coach Chris Confer describes ten guiding principles she has evolved over the years and offers specific suggestions for implementing them. Veteran coach Patricia Smith distills her years of experience into guidelines that are both informative and provocative. Winifred Findley chronicles her process for helping teachers take ownership for their classroom math teaching and learning.

Other authors, however, narrow their focus and tell how they grappled with particular questions and situations, weaving through their descriptions how they also address broader issues of their work. Robyn Silbey, for example, tackles the question of how best to ensure teachers' involvement when she teaches demonstration lessons in their classrooms. Her chapter presents the observation process she developed for teachers to use, along with the framework she follows to implement it. Leyani von Rotz's chapter describes a "math bulletin board" on which grade-level teams post examples of their students' work to develop a clearer sense of how the K–6 mathematics curriculum progresses. She explains how this broader understanding helps teachers articulate more focused expectations. Erich Zeller identifies analyzing arithmetic instruction as the focus for his school. He proposes that if teachers can achieve a shift in teaching arithmetic—the cornerstone of elementary mathematics—they can then build on this shift to think about the other areas of the math curriculum.

Establishing a collaborative culture that serves all teachers is a theme that threads throughout the entire book; for some of the authors, it is a central theme. In their chapters, Cheryl Rectanus, working in a middle school, and Stephanie Sheffield, working in an elementary school, shed light on what has (and hasn't) worked for them as they focus on enhancing teachers' talents and abilities through creating and sustaining collaborative teaching teams. Chris Confer, as math coach, collaborates with Karolyn Williams, a classroom teacher, to describe their coteaching experience and present how they tackled a particular teaching question: How do we get students to transfer what they know and understand about multiplication and division to long division? Their chapter reveals how they worked together to question and improve their instructional decisions.

In some way, most of the chapters in this book tell a tale of beginning something—a relationship, a project, or a process to impact some aspect of teaching and learning mathematics. When Marie Brigham and Kristen Berthao entered into sharing a full-time math specialist position, their initial charge was to pilot and adopt a standards-based instructional program. In their chapter, they provide rationale, direction, and results that can guide others who engage in a curriculum adoption process. Rosalyn Haberkern initiates work with a team of teachers to develop and modify a specific lesson to be taught to third graders in a lesson study cycle, a process that not only produces a model lesson but also helps the team of teachers collaborate and become interdependent.

We invite you to travel with *The Math Coach Field Guide: Charting Your Course* at hand and benefit from the experiences and reflections presented. Whether you are new to coaching or a seasoned coach, we are certain that you will find the ideas practical, stimulating, and useful as you strive to support strong mathematics instruction in your school.

Being a Successful Math Coach

Ten Guiding Principles

CHRIS CONFER

Chris Confer is the mathematics instructional coach at an elementary school in Tucson, Arizona. Her school has about 400 students. Nearly all receive free or reduced lunch, and many struggle with the issues that poverty presents. The majority of the students are second-language learners. As part of her twenty-eight-year teaching career, Chris has supported mathematics instruction at the district level for fourteen years, has supported mathematics instruction at this elementary school along with other sites for ten years, and has been a full-time mathematics specialist at this school for three years.

I remember well the day when I hesitantly agreed to become a math coach in my school, fourteen years ago. Supporting teachers and a principal on the journey to creating quality programs where children truly understood mathematics was a goal that seemed daunting to me. I felt unsure of my own abilities to do and teach mathematics, so how could I help others? It was clearly an enormous, complex task and I didn't know where to begin.

It *is* hard to know where to begin. Our goal as math coaches is not to add a little spice, salt, or pepper to the stew of mathematics instruction, but instead to alter the menu entirely. Instead of having children simply memorize isolated bits of information, children must understand and use tools of mathematics to make sense of their world.

I believe that, in the same way, teachers must have opportunities to make sense of teaching mathematics. If children are to develop these skills, which are important to their lives and to our nation, teachers cannot simply be "trained" merely to follow directions in a text. Teachers must be knowledgeable practitioners, capably using quality instructional techniques to help children from differing backgrounds and experiences become powerful mathematicians.

Over the years I learned a great deal through trial and error, the support and ideas of colleagues, and the many opportunities I had to learn about mathematics and mathematics instruction. The more I learned about how to be an effective math coach, the more I saw children, teachers, and the school community transform. And the more I witnessed this transformation, the more I fell in love with this job. In the spirit of sharing the bounty that has been offered to me, I offer you the ten principles I keep in mind as I work toward being the most effective math coach that I can be.

1. Make Good Relationships with Teachers a Priority

As a math coach I start by building solid relationships with the teachers with whom I will work. While the job of math coach implies that the school is working toward change, it's important to help teachers understand that you value the job they are presently doing in school with their students. I have come to realize that many teachers feel vulnerable when outsiders come into their classrooms, especially one who is there to encourage them to make changes. This relationship can be very fragile at first. And because the context of our lives informs our teaching, I begin by getting to know the teachers and helping them know me. I chat informally with teachers about my family and what's going on at home, and encourage them to do the same.

Specific Suggestions

◆ Help teachers in any way that you can. Remember that teachers have an enormous task. They wear many hats—social worker, psychologist, office manager; creator of materials, developer of curriculum. Furthermore, elementary teachers have to know each subject area in depth so they can meet the needs of children with widely varying abilities. Help them set up their classroom before school starts, gather materials for them, and do those little (but appreciated) things, like taking over their classes so they can get to the bathroom.

◆ Listen sympathetically to teachers' worries; they are very real. Laugh with teachers at the funny things their children do; this lightens our load. Celebrate with teachers as their children move forward; this reminds them and you why we chose this profession. Being a cheerleader is one of the most important ways that I support teachers.

◆ Understand that many teachers feel a lot of pressure from a variety of sources. Since many of these things are beyond teacher control, help them think about things that they *can* control.

◆ Talk to each teacher frequently; greet them cheerily in the halls and pop into their rooms to see how they are doing. I always try to remember that teachers are working hard to be the best teachers they can be; they do what makes sense to them according to their experiences.

◆ Honor the confidences that teachers share with you. Know that they are doing their best and that you, too, once walked in their shoes.

◆ Don't take yourself too seriously. Walls between teachers tumble down when you and they can laugh at your own mistakes.

◆ Recognize that as teachers' doors swing open and conversations begin, the school's mathematics program begins to change. Some teachers love and thrive on this change. Others may need your reassurance that they are doing good things for children, and that we're all learning together how to make things even better.

2. Work Alongside Teachers as a Coteacher, Not an Evaluator

In the same way that children learn more when they feel safe and can say what they really think, teachers are more willing to question their instruction and make changes when they feel comfortable with their math coach. This becomes difficult when teachers think they are being evaluated. I see myself as another teacher, and work to make sure that the classroom teachers see me in that same light.

This perception often does not happen naturally. Many schools are organized in hierarchies, and teachers may view administrators as the "top," teachers as the "bottom," and resource teachers as somewhere in the middle. I work hard to change this image, so that teachers see me as a colleague, not as an evaluator or someone who has special powers or privileges.

I find it helpful to move discussions away from teachers themselves and toward the learning that we teachers are doing together. I see myself as a researcher into how I can best improve my teaching practices, and I invite other teachers to think with me about instructional issues. One year I focused a lot on asking good questions, another year on developing mathematical language. I read articles, worked hard on incorporating new strategies into my lessons, and engaged teachers in conversations about my own research and what I was discovering. I soon found that these discussions permeated the entire school.

Specific Suggestions

◆ Make sure teachers know that you are their advocate, not their evaluator.

◆ Keep the same hours as teachers do. Arrive at school before the required time, and leave later than what is required.

◆ Do the same day-to-day tasks that other teachers do. Serve on committees, help with registration on the first day of school, and help out in the cafeteria from time to time.

◆ Help teachers understand that you are not there to tell people what to do, but instead have many questions about mathematics and mathematics instruction. When teachers see that you don't know everything, they feel free to begin asking questions about their own instruction. You become a peer—a colearner—rather than someone who already knows the answers.

◆ Be a researcher yourself about quality mathematics instruction. Challenge yourself to improve facets of your own teaching, such as how to better support second language learners, or how to create extensions for students who need additional challenges. Invite classroom teachers to research similar aspects in their own classrooms and to share their ideas with you. When you work in other teachers' classrooms, ask them to observe how specific changes impact student learning. For example, I might say to Ms. Tran, "Would you observe Dánica and Alejandro to see whether they understand how area is different from perimeter?" After the lesson, I would have a conversation about what she noticed, and think with her about how the lesson could be refined.

3. Begin by Working with Teachers Who Are Interested, Curious, or Open to Change About a Different Way to Teach Math

You will get the most momentum as quickly as possible by beginning with teachers who are interested in changing how they teach mathematics and who want you to work with them. By spending the majority of your time working in those classrooms and encouraging these teachers to talk to each other, you begin to create a culture of quality mathematics instruction. When teachers see others teaching differently, when they hear other teachers' excitement about their children's learning, they become interested as well. Excitement begets excitement, and change encourages more change.

Schools are systems, and changing one part of the system alters the balance and the status quo, so that the entire system can shift. Like a snowball that hurtles down a hill and gets bigger and goes faster and faster, starting with a few interested people can expand into a network of teachers engaged in professional investigations and professional discussions.

This is contrary to what many people think, and understandably so. Some believe that the teachers with the greatest needs require attention first, and schools do have the responsibility of addressing that problem. But my goal as a math coach is to affect the system, to make profound changes in *all* the staff.

Specific Suggestions

◆ Chat informally with teachers to keep informed about what they are doing with their children. This will help you see ways to support and connect with them. Some of the most powerful work I do is during those conversations in the hallways when a teacher asks a quick question, or I share an insight or ask a question of my own.

◆ Invite teachers to investigate some part of mathematics that interests them or that they see as important. For example, I might say to Mrs. López, "I see that you're working on geometry these days. I just found a copy of *The Tangram Magician*. Would you like me to bring it to your classroom and we can use it to introduce a tangram activity to your children?"

◆ Share your excitement about what you see the children doing in other teachers' classrooms. Invite teachers to become involved in the same investigation so that they become a community of learners.

◆ Help all teachers but, in the beginning at least, help them in different ways based on their individual needs. Check in with all teachers once a week to see what they need, so that all teachers know that you are available and accessible. This also keeps you up-to-date about issues that teachers are confronting.

◆ While you may plan or problem solve or find materials for all teachers, reserve a consistent block of quality time for those interested in your in-class help. Work with teachers who want you there.

◆ When you encounter resistant people, continue to be respectful, friendly, and open. Few of us learned mathematics this way, or have models for this kind of instruction. Teachers learn at different rates just as children do. And I often find I can learn from people who disagree with me; they may have a point that I need to consider.

4. Recognize That Change in Instruction Happens Primarily When Support Relates to Teachers' Specific Classroom Instructional Needs

The work I do with teachers in the classroom is the basis of how I support change in our school's mathematics programs. I rarely do demonstration lessons because teachers are more interested and engaged when we teach together. As we teach together, we encounter the real complexities of teaching, and we think through some of the hundreds of decisions that teachers have to make instantly.

Before I meet with a teacher to plan a lesson, I consider instructional techniques that will be helpful for this lesson. I know that teachers' planning time is precious, so I try to have the groundwork prepared ahead of time.

When we plan the lesson together, we begin by identifying its focus. Then we decide how we will introduce the investigation, identify how to support children during the investigation, and plan how to process, or discuss, the investigation with the children. We also identify some of the difficult vocabulary the children are likely to encounter. Then we talk about which of us will do which part of the teaching.

I usually prefer to have the teacher begin the lesson by introducing me, if necessary, and letting the children know what the focus of the lesson is, perhaps connecting it to what the children have already done with that topic. I prefer to introduce the actual investigation to the children, since I usually have had more time to think through the lesson. Once I have completed the introduction, and the teacher can see the direction of my teaching, I often ask the teacher to continue the line of questioning or the discussion.

I love the synergy that is created when the teacher and I encounter a confused student or a difficulty in a lesson, and we find that we need each other to figure out the best approach. The teacher has a lot to contribute, based on his or her understanding of teaching and the students. My own contributions stem from my focus on mathematics and teaching practices. Together we find that we are a strong team—and both of us learn!

The learning that I am constantly doing in classrooms keeps me honest in my work with teachers. I remember that there is no one "best way," no magic solution to teaching mathematics. I make sure that each year I know at least one classroom of children very well. This allows me to look at learning over the course of the year, and to help teachers deal with the hard issues such as weaving together a strong curriculum, meeting the needs of children with different levels of experiences, and assessing student learning.

Specific Suggestions

◆ Always plan with teachers before working in their classrooms. Use your school's lesson plan format but plan in additional detail. Specifically plan each part of the lesson, such as how you will introduce the lesson, how you will support students who need additional help, and how you will have the students discuss what they discovered. Clarify the roles that each of you will take during each part of the lesson. For example, Mrs. Nelson and I might plan to introduce the lesson together, or I might introduce the lesson while Mrs. Nelson observes how the students respond to my introduction.

◆ Talk with the teacher ahead of time about who will do what during the lesson. Begin the teaching so that the teacher gets a better sense of how you're approaching the lesson. Then "hand off" the lesson to the teacher. Be sure that the teacher and you feel comfortable jumping in to help each other when necessary.

◆ Chat with the teacher as the children work. Share what you notice, listen to the teacher's perceptions, and value them. Talk together about how you can support children who need help, and how you can offer certain children additional challenges. Discuss changes that you need to make as the lesson progresses.

◆ Share your excitement about children's thinking and strategies with their teacher. Help the teacher to see the children through new ideas and marvel at the different ways children think.

- Work alongside the teacher to improve instruction as you teach. Help each other to find the best questions that clarify children's thinking and misperceptions, and move them to new understandings.

- Know that your lessons are not perfect and never will be. In fact, teachers need to see that you make mistakes too! Laugh at your mistakes and learn from them—together.

- Respect teachers' different ways of organizing classrooms and the special relationship that they have built with their children. Remember that at first you are a guest and over time you will become part of this community of learners.

- Touch base with the teacher later in the day, to chat about what went well, or to have an in-depth conference. Talk about what you noticed in the children, effective questions, changes you'd make if you were to do the lesson again, and where the class might need to go next. If you have time, edit the lesson plan with these changes.

5. Provide Teachers with Ongoing Chances to Meet with Other Teachers to Be Learners of Mathematics and to Reflect on Their Instruction

I am convinced that the more mathematics I know, the more I understand how the concepts and models build a strong mathematical framework for students. The more mathematics I know, the better I see how the continuum of curriculum builds from the children's earliest mathematical understandings to more complex concepts. The better I understand this continuum, the more I can meet the needs of different students, and help them make connections between concepts so they truly make sense of mathematics.

When teachers do not understand mathematics, they tend to fall into the misunderstanding that their task is simply to cover objectives that will be tested. They believe that objectives have relatively equal importance, and that teaching happens best through simply telling the children procedures and having the children practice so they can remember. Instead, this kind of teaching leads children to fragile understandings that crumble under the weight of too many partially memorized, disconnected objectives. That is when children ask, "Do I add? Do I subtract? Just tell me what to do!"

Teachers, like children, learn more when they can talk about what they are learning. Therefore, teachers benefit from chances to discuss their ideas about teaching mathematics. Teachers need chances to attend workshops, preferably with teachers at other schools. At district-wide workshops, teachers become researchers about mathematics curriculum and best practices. They try out the activities that they will do with children and think through instructional and curriculum issues. Teachers can meet again after they have tried the lesson with their students, to share ideas and solve problems together.

But teachers can also benefit from meeting with teachers from their own site. Pairs of teachers can plan the same lesson, and end up in a dynamic discussion about teaching practices. Larger groups or the entire staff can meet to look at how particular concepts are developed throughout the grades, consistency in expectations from grade to grade, or other issues that affect that site alone.

Specific Suggestions

◆ Search out opportunities for teachers to learn mathematics. District-level workshops, where teachers can be released of classroom responsibilities for a day so they can learn mathematics and think about mathematics instruction, are best. College classes, study groups, and conferences through professional organizations such as the National Council of Teachers of Mathematics give teachers chances to learn mathematics and about mathematics instruction.

◆ Search out or create chances for teachers to come together to discuss teaching issues. These can be workshops for teachers researching mathematics instruction, book study groups, or a pair of teachers discussing student work.

◆ Look for in-depth institutes that help teachers make paradigm shifts, such as Math Solutions. These longer workshops move teachers to question what they typically do, and often are the impetus for change.

◆ Try to find ways that teachers from your school can meet with teachers from other schools. This frees teachers of their typical patterns of interactions, allowing them to think more broadly.

◆ Help teachers learn about what standardized tests do tell us and don't tell us about children. Through a curriculum focused on concepts and problem solving, children can make sense of tests—they're simply another problem to solve.

◆ When you find opportunities to learn mathematics, don't just put a note in teachers' boxes—invite them in person. Share your enthusiasm about this opportunity.

◆ Have several teachers go together to conferences or workshops, and attend with them. Some of the most effective conversations I've had with teachers took place over lunch during a workshop, or while driving to a conference.

◆ Let the teachers know that there are no simple answers, that you are still learning mathematics, that you love math, and that you enjoy teaching it.

6. Encourage Teachers to Share with Others What They Are Learning About Teaching Mathematics

Teachers become excited as they see their children grow mathematically. When teachers share their students' work, or their stories about how they helped the children, they grow professionally. Through articulating their learning to other teachers, to parents, or to their administrator, teachers better understand and recognize the value of their new instructional strategies. When teachers have an audience, they must think specifically about how they supported the children and how to verbalize the growth that they saw.

Remember that at your school site you are creating a culture of research, where new ideas do not lay stagnant but instead spread throughout the school and then to the wider world. Presenting their discoveries about teaching mathematics validates the learning that the teachers are doing and the spirit of research that you are creating at your school.

Specific Suggestions

◆ Look for informal chances for teachers to share what they know. For example, if Mr. Sánchez asks about using geoboards, I might tell him a little but then encourage him to check with Ms. Paul, who has done some great geometry investigations with them.

◆ When you give a parent workshop, invite a teacher to help—even in a small way. This allows teachers to try out a new role, and encourages them to do even more the next time.

◆ Encourage teachers to present during professional development classes or workshops and conferences. Help the teachers plan what to say or do, and offer to support them by presenting with them, or providing incidental or simply moral support.

◆ Don't overlook the many ideas for presentations that abound in day-to-day teaching. Teachers who attend conferences love to see student work and hear stories about how specific students responded to new activities or methods of instruction. Even incidents that may seem small, such as how Clarissa finally was able to use the open number line to solve a problem, provide an enjoyable yet profound focus for a workshop or conference presentation.

◆ Encourage teachers to put children's work in the hallway. Other teachers wonder what they did, and great conversations begin.

7. Communicate with Your Administrators

The better your principal understands what good mathematics instruction looks like, the more effective you can be. Help your principal understand that mathematics is the study of relationships, and that these relationships have to be constructed as children learn actively, through using concrete models or manipulatives, by talking about what they know, and by making connections.

This kind of learning is not linear and does not happen in one day. Make sure that the principal understands that complex concepts must develop over time through many experiences. The principal may observe some children's confusion and be concerned, but I explain ahead of time that this a natural part of the learning process. I tell principals that it is important to take the time to help children make sense, rather than to go forward with a superficial veneer of success that will crumble when expectations increase.

Principals frequently have read about this kind of mathematics instruction, but they may not have had the chance to learn or teach mathematics in this way. So as often as possible, invite the principal into classrooms, so he or she can see examples of quality mathematics instruction. Encourage the principal to participate with a group of children in an investigation. Just as children and teachers learn through seeing and doing, the principal needs many of these same opportunities.

Specific Suggestions

◆ Meet with the principal on a regular basis. Make sure your principal knows with whom you are working, and on what topic. Share your celebrations, both about children and about teachers' growth.

◆ Give your principal copies of articles that he or she may find helpful. Highlight specific sections that you especially want the principal to read.

◆ Recognize that principals are under tremendous pressures. Many find that it's a lonely job. Offer the same supportive, listening ear to

the principal that you offer to teachers. Honor any confidences that
a principal shares with you.

◆ Invite the principal to watch classroom lessons. For example,
when I'm coteaching in a class with children engaged in a mathematical investigation, I might slip out, find the principal, and say,
"You *have* to see the incredible strategies that Mrs. Jones's students
are using with addition!" When the principal comes in, I clearly
explain the value of what the children are doing.

◆ Share with your principal your research into quality mathematics
instruction and strategies that you and the teachers find successful.
Discuss ways to incorporate discussions about these strategies into
staff meetings.

◆ Discuss the importance of students making sense of mathematics.
Share assessments and anecdotes that show student understanding
and confusions and discuss the implications they may have.
For example, if typical fifth graders say that $\frac{1}{8}$ is larger than $\frac{1}{4}$
because 8 is larger than 4, you may explain to the principal that the
fifth-grade teachers plan to take additional time with fractions to
help students understand the foundational idea of what fractions
mean.

◆ Invite the principal to workshops, classes, and conferences. The
more mathematics that principals know, and the more they learn
about quality mathematics instruction, the better they will be able
to support their teachers.

8. Create a Mathematically Rich School Environment

It's important to spend time ensuring that the school environment is
full of mathematics. Not only do children learn from their surround-
ings, but teachers, parents, and visitors do as well.

When I work in classrooms, I try to put some children's work in
the hallways to reflect what the children learned. Next to the student

work I place a description of what the investigation was about. I also post a list of the mathematical understandings that the children were developing, in clear and simple language that parents can understand. As well, I like to include a question for children to think about as they walk by. For example, our "Life-Sized Zoo"—life-sized pictures of animals that our math club drew—has questions such as "How many tigers would equal the length of the King Cobra?"

Hallways and school gathering areas, such as the library or cafeteria, are blank slates where math coaches can offer invitations for schoolwide investigations. I currently have a centimeter height chart in the cafeteria next to the place where the children wait in line. I periodically add information about the height of school personnel in centimeters and place new challenges for the children to think about. We occasionally gather schoolwide data, such as where our students were born, and place the information in the foyer so that visitors to our school can better understand our community.

Specific Suggestions

◆ Make sure that your hallway display communicates the focus of the lesson and the mathematics that the children were learning. Keep the language clear and free of jargon. For example, "goals" may be easier for visitors to understand than "performance objectives."

◆ Capitalize on the mathematics that can happen through current events and school activities, such as fund-raising, or the number of days until a special occasion. Make hallway displays that highlight the mathematical possibilities. For example, since the student council is currently having a schoolwide food drive, I'm helping a class weigh the donated food and make a display showing how close we are to our goal.

◆ Conduct schoolwide surveys or investigations. Place the results in the hallway for everyone to read.

◆ Make available a set of mathematical games for children to use after lunch or during recess. Put a basket of counting books or books with patterns in the school entrance where people might sit. Place a simple puzzle on a table in the hallway where parents might wait with a younger sibling.

◆ When teachers attend workshops, put something that was used during the workshop, such as a chart or other display, near the workroom to remind the teachers about what they learned.

9. Remember That Parents Are an Untapped Resource

Parents are the children's first teachers. They taught their children how to talk, how to get along with others, how to share, and innumerable things about how the world functions. They are also the most important mathematics teachers the children will ever have.

Be aware that most classrooms look different from what parents experienced when they went to school. Children are talking, working in groups, using manipulatives, and writing during math class—all things that parents didn't do as children. Parents need to know why we teach in a way that is different from what they experienced when they were children.

When parents have an understanding of the value of mathematics and how mathematics is taught at school, they can better support their children's learning at home. When parents learn why mathematics classes look different, their anxiety disappears and they understand the value of the experiences their children are having at school. And when parents learn what good mathematical instruction looks like, they can be real advocates for their children in this school and in other schools.

Specific Suggestions
◆ Provide parents with workshops. Have them try out some mathematical investigations that their children are doing. By actually doing mathematics investigations, parents see the value of this kind of instruction. Explain what concepts children learn and how the concepts fit into the curriculum.

◆ Have Math Nights when parents and children can do mathematics activities together. By watching their children in action, parents see the power that children have when they own the mathematics, rather than having to memorize, forget, and memorize again. The more parents understand, the more they can support their children's learning.

◆ Be sure to help parents see that there are many ways to solve a problem, and we value children's thinking.

◆ Let parents know that it's not helpful to tell the children that they themselves were never good at math. Help parents understand that mathematics is an important door to professional careers, and that every child can be successful at math. Paint a picture of possibility.

◆ Put simple and fun mathematics problems in the school newsletter for parents to solve with their children.

◆ When teachers begin a new unit in mathematics, help them write a letter home that tells parents what their children will be learning, and things they might do at home to reinforce that learning.

◆ Help teachers select homework that reinforces what the children are learning, and that shows parents what is happening at school.

10. Surround Yourself with a Support System

Just as I suspected from the beginning, this is not a job for the faint-hearted! It is a complex one that is demanding not only intellectually, but emotionally and physically as well. A natural part of change is letting go of the old, and it's not easy to support many schools and teachers as they undergo this process.

Our job requires strong listening skills, flexibility, and the ability to understand and appreciate different viewpoints. Although I try to remember that "problems are our friends" and often lead to new ideas and growth, I often find myself wondering how to approach them. I find that I need my own sounding board, to figure out what to do.

If your district gathers math coaches on a regular basis, you are fortunate. If not, you will need to create the opportunities yourself. It's worth the effort to have a group or friend who can listen to your stories and provide you with a fresh perspective, someone with whom you can laugh or vent, and someone with whom you can think through ideas or share experiences from similar situations.

Specific Suggestions

◆ Find a colleague with the same or a similar job. Meet for coffee, and e-mail each other frequently. Although our district reorganized and eliminated our support group, several of us continue meeting regularly on our own after school hours.

◆ Read as much as you can. Outstanding educators have written books about nearly any topic that you're interested in: teaching specific strands of mathematics to specific grades; encouraging quality classroom discussions about mathematics; teaching young children mathematics; integrating mathematics with literature or science; and on and on.

◆ The National Council of Mathematics and other professional organizations provide access to a larger network through their journals, regional and local meetings, and Web sites. Attend conferences and go to workshops. Take advantage of the support you can get from being part of a nationwide group of professionals on the same path with the same goals.

Finally, know that you are on a journey that will last your entire career. It's absolutely true that the more I know, the more I see that there is to learn. I try to keep in mind that there is no end; we are never "there." It's important, therefore, to periodically look back at how far you—and your school—have come. Just as you would do when hiking up a mountain trail, stop now and then on your professional journey. Relax for a moment. Enjoy the changing view.

The Math Bulletin Board

A Vehicle for Examining
the Curriculum Across the Grades

LEYANI VON ROTZ

Leyani von Rotz served as the math coach in an elementary school, located in Emeryville, a small community tucked in between Berkeley and Oakland, California. The school serves about 450 K–6 students, with the student body made up primarily of African American, East Indian, and Latino children. There are twenty classroom teachers. Before assuming this position, Leyani had taught kindergarten and first grade at the school for five years.

In 2000, I became the math coach at my school. This was a new position for the school, which meant that I had the responsibility—and opportunity—for making decisions about how I would fulfill the role. After five years, I am still feeling my way, relying on trial and error, support from my principal and superintendent, collaboration with the school's language arts coach, feedback from the teachers, and my ongoing classroom experiences.

We're fortunate at my school to have time during the day for teachers to meet in grade-level teams to work on math. Last year these meetings were scheduled once a week; now we meet every other week. These meetings have been wonderful for giving teachers the chance to plan together and discuss the results of their teaching from the previous weeks.

One of the early discoveries I made from these meetings was that the teachers, in general, didn't have a clear sense of how the K–6 mathematics curriculum developed over the grades. During our meetings, they focused their attention on their own grade-level needs with little attention to the concepts and skills that might have preceded their grade level, and what might follow. Because of this, I set as one of my goals to help teachers develop a perspective of children's mathematical development across the grades.

To address this goal, I cleared the bulletin board in my office for a display of samples of student work from each of the school's grade levels. My plan was to ask each grade-level team of teachers to select children's work to post from their own classes. Then I would give time in all of the grade-level meetings for teachers to view, analyze, and discuss the work displayed from other grades. My purpose as a math coach was to get teachers to really look at and think about their students' work and to engage in discussions with their colleagues about what they expected and how they got the results they wanted.

As a first step, I introduced the idea of the bulletin board by giving grade-level teams time to talk about what they would hope to learn from seeing student work from other grades. Terri, a fourth-grade teacher, gave a typical response. She said, "I want to see what my students will be expected to do next year."

Raschelle, a kindergarten teacher, said, "I'd love to see what my students from past years are doing now."

Cecile, a second-grade teacher, said, "I want to see the kinds of things that the kindergarten and first-grade teachers are doing to get students ready for second grade."

After these discussions, I asked the teachers at each grade to come up with an assignment that they thought would communicate to the rest of the teachers in the school about the mathematics the children in their classes were learning. In some grade-level discussions, teachers agreed quickly, while in others, teachers spent a good deal of time discussing and deliberating. These discussions in themselves were useful because they focused teachers on what was important about the curriculum in their grades.

For these initial discussions, I didn't specify a particular area of the mathematics curriculum, and I was curious to see what the different teams would choose. All grade-level groups decided to focus on number and operations, which was useful later for making comparisons across the grades. (Looking back, I think it might have been useful to establish this focus at the onset to ensure that there would be a common focus in the students' papers.)

I then told the teachers that they would each give their team's assignment to their own class and bring the student work to our next meeting sorted into two categories: *Meets Standard* or *Needs More Instruction*. To help teachers sort the work, I asked them to think about the criteria they would use for deciding that a paper met the standard for the assignment. I encouraged them to think of the papers in the second category as needing more instruction instead of being wrong, and to think about what they might do next for the students who needed further teaching.

At the following grade-level meetings, to begin the discussion about the work the teachers had brought, I asked each teacher to select an example of student work from each of the two categories and prepare to explain why it belonged there. I also asked them to choose a third piece of work that they were unsure of or had questions about.

In all of the meetings, it turned out that teachers had different ideas of what *Meets Standard* meant. It was helpful for teachers to have a chance to discuss these differences. For example, some teachers listed "correct answer" as one of the criteria for *Meets Standard;* others emphasized "multiple representations" but didn't list "correct answer"; and others listed "neatness" or "clarity" as criteria. During the discussions teachers learned from one another and were able, with time, to come up with and write down criteria that they could all agree on. Finally, I asked them, as a team, to choose two pieces of work to represent their grade level: one for *Meets Standard* and another for *Needs More Instruction*.

For example, the fourth-grade team chose an assignment from *Teaching Arithmetic: Lessons for Extending Multiplication* (Wickett and

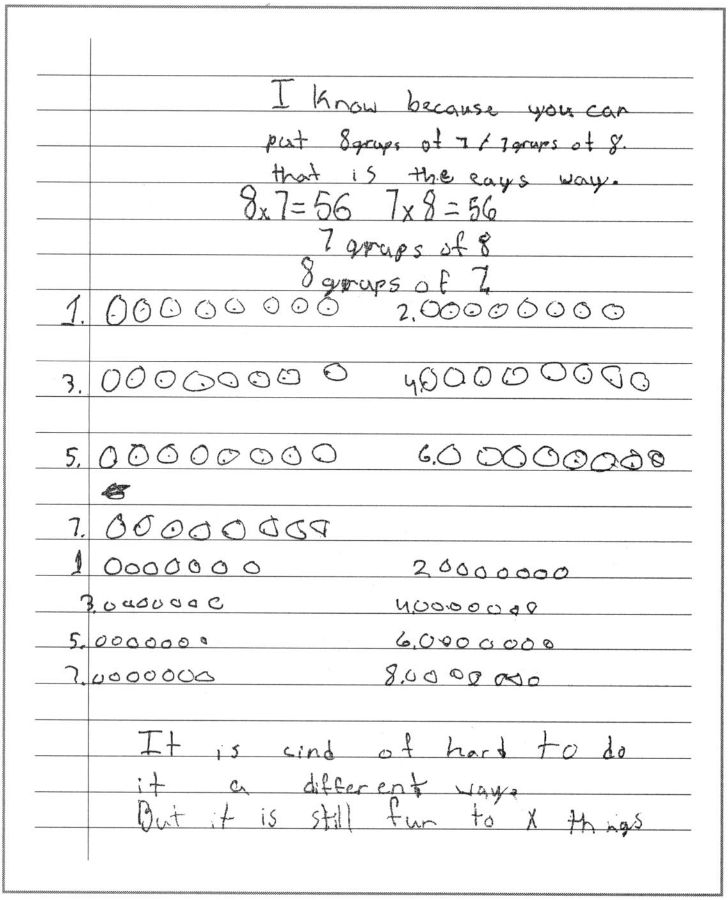

I know because you can put 8 grups of 7 / 7 grups of 8. that is the eays way.

$8 \times 7 = 56$ $7 \times 8 = 56$

7 grups of 8
8 grups of 7

1. O O O O O O O O   2. O O O O O O O O

3. O O O O O O O O   4. O O O O O O O O O

5. O O O O O O O O O   6. O O O O O O O O O

7. O O O O O O O O O

1. O O O O O O O   2. O O O O O O O

3. O O O O O O O   4. O O O O O O O O

5. O O O O O O O   6. O O O O O O O

7. O O O O O O O   8. O O O O O O O

It is cind of hard to do it a different ways. But it is still fun to X things

FIG. 2–1 *This student represented multiplication in a variety of ways, including grouping.*

Burns 2001). Their prompt was: *Using words, pictures, and numbers, show as many ways as you can to solve 8 × 7.* The team chose Sara's paper (Figure 2–1) as an example of *Meets Standard* and described the criteria: *Student represents multiplication in a variety of ways, including grouping, and gets correct answer.* They chose Peter's paper (Figure 2–2) as an example of needing more instruction. They described the criteria: *Student shows only one strategy and is not accurate.*

The descriptions led to further debate. What if students showed one strategy and were accurate? What if they used a variety of ways

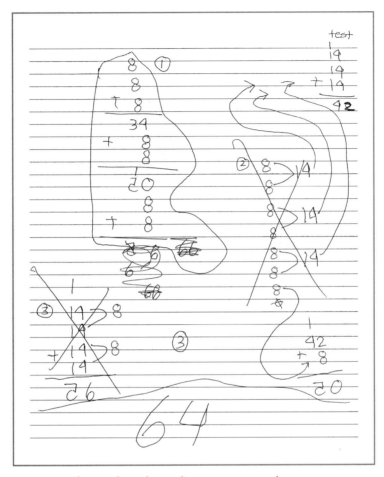

FIG. 2–2 *This student showed one strategy and was not accurate.*

but got the wrong answer? This discussion highlighted the complex task of evaluating student work and especially how hard it is to come up with a foolproof definition for a "good paper."

The kindergarten team had chosen student work from the Counting Jar activity they were doing in the TERC unit *Mathematical Thinking in Kindergarten* (Economopoulos and Russell 1995b) (Figures 2–3 and 2–4). They described the criteria they would use for all of the papers that fit the *Meets Standard* category: *Students accurately represent number of items in counting jar.* This team decided that

FIG. 2–3 *These students accurately represented the number of items in the counting jar. One student showed self-correction.*

they needed to show several samples of student work from this assignment for *Meets Standard* in order to accurately describe the criteria they identified. They felt that the evidence of self-correction was valuable information, and they chose a paper that showed this so teachers at other grade levels could examine it. Also, they added to the criteria: *Student shows self-correction.* For the work needing more instruction, the kindergarten team wrote: *Students do not accurately represent number of items in counting jar.*

The bulletin board became filled with the samples of student work. For each piece of work, I typed a caption with the description the teachers had come up with. Then, when I met with grade-level teams, I began each meeting by asking my favorite question: "What do you notice?" Asking this question opens up a discussion and gives me

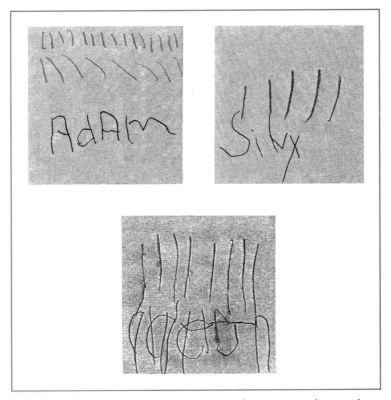

FIG. 2–4 *These students did not accurately represent the number of items in the counting jar.*

insights into the kinds of things that teachers find of interest and importance.

"I can see how the work is changing and getting more sophisticated over time," said Megan, a sixth-grade teacher.

The fifth-grade team was surprised to see that they were doing almost the same work that the fourth-grade team was doing. The fifth grade was also working on multiplication but with slightly larger numbers. Charise, a fifth-grade teacher, said, "Wow. I didn't realize my students had this last year. Maybe I can move a little faster."

When Eileen, a first-grade teacher, looked at the papers posted, she said, "Last year, I thought my students couldn't do much, but now I see there's a huge difference between what they can accomplish in kindergarten and what they're doing now."

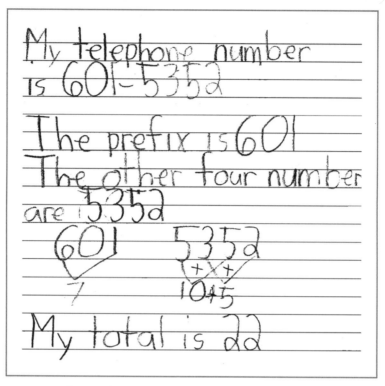

FIG. 2–5 *This student correctly added his phone number using a strategy called doubles.*

Teachers also got lesson ideas from each other. The second-grade team loved the phone number activity the third grade had done (see Tank and Zolli 2001). (See Figure 2–5.) Laura commented, "What a good idea! It's so simple—they just add up the digits in their telephone numbers. I'm going to ask the teachers how they introduced it."

The work also generated questions. The kindergarten team didn't understand why the first-grade team had labeled work as *Needs More Instruction* when it seemed correct to them (Figure 2–6) (see TERC unit *Mathematical Thinking at Grade 1* [Economopoulos and Russell 1995a]). The first-grade team's description for the paper was: *Student shows correct solution using pictures.*

"I don't get it," said Raschelle. "The paper is right."

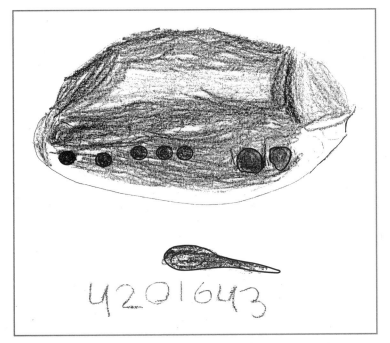

FIG. 2–6 *This student showed a correct solution using pictures.*

"Yeah, but read the description of the *Meets Standard* paper," said Malcolm. "It looks like they wanted more than just a picture." For that paper (Figure 2–7), the first-grade team had written: *Student shows correct solution using numbers, pictures, and words.*

Teachers commented on their need to spend more time figuring out what they expected from their students' work before they taught a lesson. Many times during the process of analyzing the student work, teachers said that they wanted more out of the work but they realized that they had not been explicit enough in their directions.

"This process really helped me see that I need to talk to my colleagues more. I had no idea we had such different ideas of what a good paper was," said Peggy, a second-grade teacher.

"I can't give them a bad grade on a paper if I didn't tell them up front what I wanted," commented Charise.

Twice more during the school year we repeated the process of posting students' math work, and each time the bulletin board was

FIG. 2–7 *This student showed a correct solution using numbers, pictures, and words.*

finished, teachers were excited to see the results. "It's so exciting to see what other grades are doing. It's like a little field trip around the school," said Kris, a fourth-grade teacher. Also, each time we repeated the process, teachers found it easier to describe their criteria for *Meets Standard*.

My goal in creating the bulletin board was to help teachers deepen their understanding of students' mathematical learning across the grades.

After one year of this process, I noticed that teachers became more aware of and interested in the work of the children in their colleagues' classes, both at their own grade level and at other grade levels. Also, the communication among the teachers about the math they're teaching increased. I expect that over the coming years, the bulletin-board process will continue to build teachers' perspectives about their students' progress and our school's math program.

References

Economopoulos, Karen, and Susan Jo Russell. 1995a. *Mathematical Thinking at Grade 1.* Palo Alto, CA: Dale Seymour.

———. 1995b. *Mathematical Thinking in Kindergarten.* Palo Alto, CA: Dale Seymour.

Tank, Bonnie, and Lynne Zolli. 2001. *Teaching Arithmetic: Lessons for Addition and Subtraction, Grades 2–3.* Sausalito, CA: Math Solutions Publications.

Wickett, Maryann, and Marilyn Burns. 2001. *Teaching Arithmetic: Lessons for Extending Multiplication, Grades 4–5.* Sausalito, CA: Math Solutions Publications.

Coaching a Middle School Math Team

Creating a Collaborative Learning Community

CHERYL RECTANUS

Cheryl Rectanus is the middle school mathematics coordinator and a secondary mathematics specialist in a large, urban school district in Portland, Oregon, responsible for coordinating professional development for teachers, school math teams, administrators, and paraprofessionals. This chapter describes how she coached a middle school math team at a school with one of the lowest student achievement scores in the state, where 74 percent of the students receive free or reduced lunch, and more than forty-five languages are spoken. Cheryl taught elementary and middle school in self-contained, departmentalized, and mixed-age settings for fifteen years.

I first began working with the math team at a middle school in my district several years ago, when I was just new to my position as a district math coordinator. The school was characterized by low socioeconomic status (SES), frequent principal and staff turnover, and a high rate of student mobility. It did not have a math coach, either full- or part-time, and the principal asked me for help by filling that role. There were six math teachers on the team—Sally, Bette, Gerald, Lisa, Jose, and Tia (not their real names). Their differing beliefs about how students learn mathematics and about how to teach mathematics presented several challenges.

Sally was a dynamic teacher who was committed to connecting with her students to support their math learning. Her students were engaged and enthusiastic learners in the classroom and performed adequately on standardized achievement measures. Sally's teaching practice was consistent with national recommendations.

Bette was new to the staff but had been teaching math in the district for many years. Like Sally, she was familiar with the national recommendations for teaching and learning mathematics and talked about embracing them. However, her classroom practice was inconsistent with her talk. In her lessons, Bette usually told students what to do and how to do it; rarely were students expected to solve nonroutine problems or to explain their reasoning during discussions. Bette made occasional comments to me and others on the math team that revealed some of her beliefs and assumptions about her students. For example, when referring to her poor, nonwhite students, Bette once said, "Well, their parents don't care about education and those kids just mess around in class and hang out when they're not in school, so what am I supposed to do? I can't solve that problem!" She was not convinced that every student can learn.

Bette also privately commented to me that she thought the other teachers on the math team—especially Gerald and Sally—were poor teachers. She was fairly domineering and saw herself in a leadership position. Her abrasive style led to conflicts with others on the math team, especially with Sally. Many tensions simmered below the surface, and, at times, the conflicts bubbled over into outright hostility.

Lisa and Gerald were veteran teachers at the school. Both quietly tried to stay out of the conflicts between Sally and Bette, but were sometimes drawn in by Bette's dominating arguments. Rounding out the team were Jose and Tia, two young, inexperienced teachers who were struggling with planning and teaching lessons and with classroom management.

I knew all of these math teachers before I began working with them as a math team. I had worked with some on various committees when I was still a classroom teacher. Others I had met at district-wide professional development days. So when their principal contacted me to share that the team was having difficulty getting along and asked if I would please step in and help at an upcoming meeting I agreed, even though "fixing" the team was not a role that I wanted to play. I talked with the principal about the culture of the math team, his goals for them, and how I might begin working with the team. He felt strongly that I should facilitate the meeting since I was an "outsider." His main goal was for Sally in particular to share her teaching practices so the rest of the team could "do as Sally does." From our conversation, I realized that he thought having Sally say the right words could help others change. Thus the way that he had structured the meeting encouraged advice giving, or a platform where Sally could espouse her positions. It did not provide opportunities for collaboratively inquiring about one's own teaching practice.

While the principal's plan didn't feel especially promising or comfortable to me, he was firm in his decision to have the meeting. We agreed that he would arrange half-day substitutes for the math teachers to meet together with me.

On the appointed afternoon, the six math teachers and I gathered in a school conference room. I had decided to begin by finding out what concerns they had in common, hoping to establish some common ground that would allow us to tackle more contentious issues, so I asked each to tell his or her understanding about why we were there. There were six different answers! Further discussion did produce common ground. They all were concerned that students' work completion rate was, by most indications, dismal. We generated a list of possible reasons why students do and do not complete work. It was interesting to note who offered each explanation because it gave me a window into their beliefs and assumptions about teaching, learning, students, and their families. The conversation turned next to how to address the issue of work completion. The team members had many ideas that they shared with one another. While on the surface the team was getting along, not surprisingly the meeting had actually deteriorated into advice giving rather than collaborative inquiry. Each of the teachers at the table had a position to defend, which they did with great enthusiasm. The principal dropped in and nodded as he heard Sally sharing how she dealt with students who did not complete work. Seeming satisfied, he left shortly afterward.

At the next meeting, about a month later, the team continued with the format they had begun at the first meeting: plopping a concern on the table and sharing what to do about it. While the teachers appeared happy to report their ideas, after the second meeting, they felt that they no longer needed to meet. The format was addressing no one's needs.

As I look back at my first experience in working with the school's math team, I realize that I made several mistakes. The first was not to press the principal about the initial plan; this reflected my ambivalence about disagreeing with a principal about a particular course of action for a school. The decision to meet was the principal's agenda; it was not cocreated by the team. We didn't have a clear purpose for meeting or collaborating. We didn't explicitly address norms for interaction, so when conversations became heated, there was nothing to refer to. The structure of the meeting did not facilitate making a collaborative effort toward improving our teaching practices.

Several years passed between my initial ineffective work with the math team and my current work with them. In that time, I learned a great deal more about professional learning communities, their impact on teachers' instructional practice and student learning, and how they can change ways that teachers work together in a school. Professional learning communities are generally characterized by:

- ◆ *shared norms and values,* where participants commit to working toward attaining common goals through inquiry based on public reflection;

- ◆ *collaboration,* where participants engage together in an ongoing process that builds trust and positive relationships as they share struggles, expertise, support, and leadership;

- ◆ *a collective focus on student learning,* centering the group's work on how their teaching affects student learning and finding effective ways to address students' needs;

◆ *deprivatized practice,* or the idea that rather than teaching behind closed doors, teachers need to share their problems of practice with one another through processes such as lesson study, examining student work, video or written narrative cases, peer observation, and so on; and

◆ *reflective dialogue,* where the dialogue is based on data such as artifacts of classroom practice, including student work samples, video clips of a lesson, data collected during lesson study observations, and so forth. (See Louis, Kruse, and Marks 1996.)

With my new knowledge, I began working again with this middle school's team. There was now a new principal. Sally, Jose, and Lisa had taken jobs at other schools, but Bette, Gerald, and Tia were still on the team, joined by Louisa, a first-year teacher, and Marlene. Also, Gerald had taken on a leadership position, acting as a liaison between the school and a district math project, and he was eager to practice his new learning about leadership with the team. As part of the project, he agreed to meet with me to plan the school's first math team meeting of the year.

When I met with Gerald, we talked about the negative history that some of the math team shared. Gerald was particularly concerned that Bette would hijack the agenda as she had done at previous meetings. We agreed that if we wanted to change the culture of the group, it would first be necessary to set up protocols and structures that would support respectful communication. We discussed how dysfunctional groups tend to resist using protocols, and realized that the way Gerald chose to present the protocols would also be essential. Gerald said that he had studied some of these ideas from *Leadership Capacity for Lasting School Improvement* (Lambert 2003), *The Power of Protocols* (McDonald et al. 2003) and *The Facilitator's Book of Questions* (Allen and Blythe 2004); he'd tried having his students use a "go-around" protocol and liked how it improved communication in his math classroom.

We were both aware that how Gerald facilitated would set a tone for future meetings, and thus it was important to carefully consider how each agenda item would play out. And finally, we explored possible goals and ways of accomplishing them, talked about facilitation, and together made a detailed plan for the meeting.

During the first meeting, Gerald reminded the team that studies show that when teachers participate in collaborative learning communities focused on teaching and learning, student achievement increases. He noted that in past years, when the math team met, there wasn't a good balance between a focus on teaching practice and on business items—the team usually discussed business, but not what they did in the classroom each day. Gerald explained that he knew that each person there had effective practices as well as struggles to share about his or her teaching. Today, the team would decide how to get started this year, including setting norms; determining a decision-making process; deciding on roles that members of the math team would need to play during each meeting; addressing immediate issues; and finally, formulating agenda items for the next meeting.

Gerald also explained that at future meetings, we would look at a variety of data sources about student learning. Using that information, we'd set goals for this year and would think about what we needed to learn to achieve them, giving careful consideration to how we would know that we were making progress toward our goals.

The team began by talking about how they wanted to interact with one another during their meetings by creating group norms. Gerald asked us to consider the following: "To ensure a safe and productive learning environment, we agree to . . ." He consciously decided to have each person initially work alone, silently, and in writing. Gerald felt that writing would encourage the teachers to reflect, which is something he wanted to promote at each meeting. By first reflecting alone, the members would have the opportunity to collect and organize their thoughts without the potential interference of others' ideas. As well, Gerald wanted to model a technique that could be used in the classroom. Specifically, he thought it would be helpful for students to have the same kind of time and space to reflect on problems posed by the teacher before talking with others about the problems and their strategies for approaching them.

After a few minutes for personal reflection, Gerald asked each person in turn to share one thing from her list while he wrote the suggestions verbatim on chart paper. He deliberately did not change their words to send the message that what each person had to say was important and that the job of the facilitator was not to impose what *he thought* should go on the paper, but to capture accurately what each participant had to offer. Gerald and I had also discussed this when we met before the meeting to plan his facilitation moves.

Gerald continued this process, going around the table and eliciting one idea from each participant in turn, until all ideas had been shared and recorded. Again, his choice of a "go-around, one-person-one-idea-at-a time" protocol was a deliberate way to ensure equitable participation by all. It also enforced the message that each participant had the right to speak as well as the responsibility to share the airtime equitably.

Gerald next asked the group if there was anything on the list that they absolutely couldn't agree to. Louisa remarked, "I'm in agreement with all of the ideas on our list, but I think it's a pretty long list and we could probably combine some things." Everyone nodded in agreement. So Gerald asked us to see which ideas on the list overlapped or could be combined in some way to avoid duplication. It was a good task to assign because in the process of doing this, we each had a chance to further explain what various norms meant to us, thus helping the group create shared meaning about the ideas. We generated the following list, and it was clear from the group's nonverbal communication that everyone was satisfied with it:

To ensure a safe and productive learning environment, we agree to:

- Give mutual respect.
- Give everyone an equal voice.
- Use protocols when needed.
- Disagree, but not to undermine consensus decisions.
- Disagree with ideas, not personalities.
- Say the hard things that need to be said directly and respectfully to one another, not behind others' backs.
- Presume positive intentions.
- Make decisions based on the best interests of students.
- Meet weekly for one hour before school starts.
- Begin and end on time.
- Share facilitation and time keeping; Cheryl is the recorder.
- Set the agenda for the next meeting at the end of each meeting.

Gerald moved on to the second item on the agenda, which was to determine a decision-making process. He started by saying that while we presumed positive intentions on each person's part, we needed to have a process in place for when decision making becomes tough. He asked the group what methods they'd experienced in other meetings, and several participants shared their ideas. I noted that they were taking turns and listening carefully and attentively to one another, clearly enacting their new norms. The group quickly came to consensus that they would use a thumb up (yes, I can live with the decision), thumb held sideways (neutral), thumb down (I don't like it) method. Furthermore, the group agreed that if someone showed a thumb down, the group would keep talking about the issue until there was consensus.

Next we moved on to discussing roles. The group was familiar with the idea of sharing facilitation and recording since these were practices commonly used throughout the district, although they hadn't done much of this as a math team. Gerald told the group that in his leadership work, he learned that it was helpful in groups for everyone to take on various roles to facilitate efficient communication and to share responsibility for the smooth functioning of the team. The group brainstormed various roles that they might enact and agreed that facilitation and timekeeping would rotate among team members. Some indicated that they were uncomfortable with the idea of facilitating and I told the team that I would meet with each person who was to be the facilitator for the next meeting so he or she wouldn't have to do the planning alone. As the year went on I imagined that they'd meet with one another to plan together when I couldn't be there. I also explained that as we mutually thought through the issues of facilitating these meetings, their teaching experiences would inform their work in the classroom. I wanted to help the group begin to draw parallels between what it means to facilitate learning in the classroom and what it means to do the same with one's colleagues.

The group also decided that when I was in attendance, I would take notes for the group so they could all concentrate on participating. I agreed to record the minutes and send them to the team and the principal. We decided that we would keep the principal in the loop by sending her the meeting notes and giving her a standing invitation to the weekly meetings.

After addressing some of the typical issues that come up during the first few weeks of school, it was time to set the agenda for the next meeting. The group agreed that a timed agenda would be set at each meeting five minutes prior to the end of the meeting. The first item would always be business/reports; the second item would be old business; the third, new business. The written agenda would be included in the minutes of the prior meeting. I was not surprised that the team decided on the words old and new "business" rather than "learning," but I kept quiet at that point. I knew that there would be many opportunities in the future to return to what Gerald had described earlier: the team did a good job handling "business items" but spent practically no time at all examining their teaching practice.

When Gerald and I met later to debrief the meeting, we both agreed that even though using protocols didn't always feel "natural," in retrospect, their use allowed the group to speak civilly to one another and get important work done.

Before the second meeting, I met with the new facilitator, Marlene, to plan it. We reflected on the first meeting and thought that at the beginning of the second it would be important to do a brief activity to refocus the group on the norms for interaction. Marlene decided to ask the group how many of the agreements they could remember from our first meeting without looking at their notes. We talked about why it would be significant to touch on the norms at each meeting for the first several months to help participants internalize them. We didn't want them to become a nice list that was tucked in a notebook, never again to see the light of day. Marlene also decided that it would be a good idea to ask the group if there was anything we had left out that we wanted to add to the list. Finally, she decided to ask the group to talk about how they thought we did with our norms at the first meeting. Were there any that we needed to work on?

During the planning meeting with Marlene, I noted that the team had agreed to rotate roles but we hadn't actually discussed or agreed on what those roles would mean. What was the job of the facilitator, exactly? What sorts of things should the recorder capture? Should the minutes include who said what or should comments be anonymous? How would notes be amended if they were inaccurate? How would the timekeeper help move things along without being intrusive? What would happen if team members wanted to add something to the agenda that had been set at the previous meeting? We decided that these structural things should be addressed at the second meeting. The emphasis during these first few meetings was definitely on "business," but I knew that the team had to develop trust in one another and in the protocols before they would be willing to open their teaching practices to public scrutiny.

I attended every meeting for the first ten weeks. The teachers generally treated me as a member of the team, and I followed the same norms as the rest of the team. During those ten weeks, I met with the team member who was going to facilitate the next meeting to support that teacher in thinking through issues of facilitation. We always made time afterward to debrief. For many on the team, facilitating was intimidating, and all expressed that meeting ahead of time to plan and after the meeting to debrief was helpful. The first several meetings went relatively well. Participants were respectful of one another and actually took care of many agenda items, although to me the meetings felt overly structured and again, focused solely on business issues. In retrospect, the initial somewhat rigid structure was probably necessary; while the major conflict between Bette and Sally was gone, the team, and especially Gerald, were still somewhat wary of Bette.

A few weeks into the year, we had analyzed a variety of data sources about student needs and it was time to determine the team's focus for the year. Tia was to facilitate, and she asked me to co-facilitate that part of the meeting with her. She noted that the team was functioning better than it ever had. The group had norms for interaction and followed them. Agenda items were raised and dealt with respectfully and efficiently. But Tia recognized that while the data showed that many students were struggling, the team really wasn't putting their teaching practices on the table. She saw that the math teachers could attend the meetings each week but not examine what it is they do every day and how that affects students and student learning. Together we developed a plan to attempt to do just that. We wanted to raise awareness and talk about our beliefs and assumptions about the nature of math, students, and learning to begin examining how they influence classroom teaching and learning.

At the next meeting, we noted that based on the data from the previous week, many students had significant needs with respect to math achievement. We explained that this year, my role would be to press the team to reflect collaboratively on both their teaching and students' learning, but always with support. We told the team that we most likely would create cognitive dissonance or disequilibrium about teaching practices, but that our goal was to focus on what each team member needed to learn or do differently in the classroom to meet students' needs. I emphasized that we were not going to worry about the things we couldn't control, such as class size or students' backgrounds, but on the things within our control.

Joining us that day was Tia's student teacher, Lucy. We asked the team to write down all the things that were driving them crazy about their classes and students, and to phrase them as questions. "For example," I said, "if it really gets in the way that some of your students haven't yet developed efficient ways to compute with fractions, don't write, *My kids can't compute with fractions.* Instead, phrase it as a question that involves you, such as, *How can I support my students in developing efficient ways to compute with fractions?*"

The room fell silent as everyone began writing. After a few minutes, Louisa, the first-year teacher, burst into tears and fled the room. It was an awkward moment. I felt terrible that Louisa had become upset during this process, but fortunately she returned soon. I chose not to address the incident but moved forward and asked the teachers to identify their primary concern and to share that concern in turn.

During our planning session, Tia and I had deliberately decided to ask Lucy to begin the sharing. Lucy had attended several meetings before, and her comments often contained a thoughtful and reflective tone; we hoped the others would follow.

"How do I know that I've reached as many students as possible?" Lucy began. She went on to talk eloquently and honestly about her struggles to meet the needs of each student and her feelings of inadequacy. Tia shared next. She too spoke from her heart, focusing on her challenges with classroom management. Louisa followed, talking through her tears as she shared her fears and struggles. What happened as each person spoke was remarkable—the empathy in the room was palpable. Others on the team had tears in their eyes as each member spoke. Sharing their vulnerabilities as teachers shifted the culture of the team.

Not surprisingly, after this emotional meeting, the next meeting was "business as usual." Schools are highly resistant to change, and the pull toward what was "normal" was understandable and safe. But two weeks later, I again nudged the team. We talked about the needs the teachers had expressed and crafted a common question around which to organize our learning for the year: "How do we differentiate our instruction to best meet the needs of all of our students?" We discussed how we might begin thinking about our question and spent time developing shared meaning about the words *differentiation, instruction,* and *all students.* The team agreed that there were a number of ways we could begin: we could read a case study, examine videotape of teachers teaching, engage in a lesson study, learn more mathematics ourselves, or examine student work.

After some discussion, they decided to learn more math together. This idea made sense for several reasons. First, learning math together would immerse the teachers in what it is like to be a learner. (This would help them understand what it feels like from the students' perspective.) Also, learning together would help the team develop a vision for what a classroom that reflects best practices—including differentiation—in math looks like and how it operates.

The team asked me to take responsibility for facilitating since I had more time in my schedule for planning. We agreed that I would do math with them periodically; they needed time in between these meetings to address the many needs typical in any school. I structured several learning experiences focused on fraction operations (especially division of fractions) that we implemented over the course of the school year. I used some of the activities in *Knowing and Teaching Elementary Mathematics* (Ma 1999) to help teachers expand their content knowledge and think about pedagogy that supports student learning.

At a district math leaders meeting in the spring, Gerald spoke eloquently about how the math team at his school had changed this year. They had become collaborative because the professional development work was essentially bottom-up. He reported, "Nobody was telling us what we had to do; but we're meeting now because we want to—it meets a need for all of us when we can talk about our teaching together. Best of all, it's paying off in the classroom. Kids are happier, teachers are happier, and the students are achieving more than they ever have in the past."

The following week at the school's math team meeting, I asked Gerald if he would be willing to share with the rest of the team what he had reported at the district meeting. "Sure!" he replied enthusiastically and repeated his comments.

"I'd have to agree," added Marlene, smiling. "I thought I knew everything there was to know about teaching math, but I learned so much this year. It wouldn't have happened if we didn't have this safe environment to say to each other, 'Hey, you know, I really don't get it about how to divide fractions; can you help?'"

Louisa added, "I wouldn't have made it through this year if it weren't for all of you. My student teaching experience was in a school where the kids and parents were all involved and excited about learning and this school is so different. Without being able to talk through with you the pros and cons of different ways to structure my program and think about how it impacts kids, I'd probably have quit in October. I'm really grateful to you all."

Bette was uncharacteristically silent. Of all the members on the team, she probably had changed the least from our year of working together. She still wanted to be in charge of everything, still was convinced that her way was best, and still attempted to hijack the agenda, although the team was better about not letting her get away with it. But I am an optimist and know that significant change takes time. The team really has just begun to develop the trust in one another that is needed to be honest about our problems of practice with our colleagues.

References

Allen, David, and Tina Blythe. 2004. *The Facilitator's Book of Questions: Tools for Looking Together at Student and Teacher Work.* New York: Teachers College Press.

Lambert, Linda. 2003. *Leadership Capacity for Lasting School Improvement.* Alexandria, VA: Association for Supervision and Curriculum Development.

Louis, Karen S., Sharon D. Kruse, and Helen M. Marks. 1996. "Schoolwide Professional Community." In *Authentic Achievement: Restructuring Schools for Intellectual Quality,* ed. F. M. Newmand et al., 179–203. San Francisco: Jossey-Bass.

Ma, Liping. 1999. *Knowing and Teaching Elementary Mathematics: Teachers' Understanding of Fundamental Mathematics in China and the United States.* Mahwah, NJ: Lawrence Erlbaum.

McDonald, Joseph P., Nancy Mohr, Alan Dichter, and Elizabeth C. McDonald. 2003. *The Power of Protocols: An Educator's Guide to Better Practice.* New York: Teachers College Press.

Helping Reluctant Teachers

Facing the Challenge of Providing Support

STEPHANIE SHEFFIELD

Stephanie Sheffield is the instructional specialist for math and science in a nine-hundred-student pre-K–5 school outside of Houston, Texas. Her school has the largest elementary ESL (English as a second language) population in the school district, with more than seventeen different languages spoken in students' homes. Stephanie has taught first, third, fourth, and fifth grade during her twenty-five years of teaching.

As the instructional specialist for math and science in my building, my job includes providing staff development, helping new teachers, teaching model lessons, and working with grade-level teams to plan instruction. It is an expectation at our school that grade-level teams will plan together and we believe that collaboration creates stronger instruction for children. And while individual teachers make their own instructional choices about the lessons they teach for their own classes, many teachers find support in staying at about the same point in the curriculum as the other teachers at their grade level.

Our district curriculum is based on our state standards and expectations. We live with a high-stakes state-mandated test in grades 3 through 5, which is based on those standards. The district provides us with a scope and sequence, which specifies the sequence of units to teach and identifies resources and materials to which teachers in our district have access. Within this framework, teachers are free to choose the activities and experiences they think are best for their students.

As part of my job I plan with teams of teachers in each grade level. Some teams plan every week, while some do longer-range planning and meet every two or three weeks. Sometimes teachers on these teams are ready and eager to work with me. They are anxious to hear about new ideas and resources and interested in having me visit their classrooms. Other teachers are more reluctant to receive input or suggestions.

What both groups have in common—the teams that are eager to learn and grow and the teams that are hesitant about receiving help for their mathematics instruction—is their desire to do the best they can for their students. My role is to help all teachers teach effectively. This requires different strategies and techniques for eager and reluctant teachers. In this chapter I will focus on those teachers who are hesitant to change and need additional support, direction, and encouragement to examine and reflect on their mathematics instruction.

It is important to understand why reluctant teachers are fearful of change. Over the years, I've noticed several characteristics common to these teachers. In recognizing them, I've become more understanding of their reluctance to consider changes and more effective in working with them successfully. The characteristics these teachers share typically include:

- ◆ discomfort with standards-based mathematics curriculum;
- ◆ concern about how students will do on standardized tests if they try something new;
- ◆ fear that if they try something new it will take more time than they are willing to give;
- ◆ concern about classroom control issues if they allow students to work together and use manipulatives;
- ◆ worry that moving away from the traditional textbook will require mathematical knowledge beyond their expertise; and
- ◆ discomfort being observed as they teach.

These characteristics are based on real concerns teachers have. My role is to understand their concerns and, at the same time, find ways to provide the "nudge and support" to help them focus on their mathematics instruction. I keep several broad goals in mind throughout the year when working with hesitant teachers. I try to:

develop their trust;

develop friendly working relationships;

empower them to try new things;

help them learn to make instructional decisions based on their students' needs; and

facilitate their learning more math for themselves.

In addition to these large, somewhat intangible goals, I also work to establish specific, concrete goals with clear outcomes. I help reluctant teachers by:

helping with classroom setup;

planning lessons together; and

modeling through demonstration lessons.

Helping with Classroom Setup

I find that a good way to support hesitant teachers at the beginning of the year is to offer help as they set up their classrooms. I start by helping them arrange their furniture so students can work cooperatively in small groups or in pairs. We set up a meeting space in the room, with wall space nearby for posting a calendar and a math vocabulary wall. Together we identify an area where the teacher will work with small groups of students. Then I help them identify a storage system that will provide easy access to math manipulatives for the students and the teacher. Some teachers organize materials in clear plastic shoebox-size boxes with lids, so that students can see the contents of each box.

Others use baskets bought at a dollar store, or small plastic containers collected at home. I explain that students need to be able to identify the contents of the boxes, either by seeing the material, by reading the name of the material, or by seeing a picture of it. During the first weeks of school, I also visit classrooms to help teachers as they set their expectations with their students about how and when math manipulatives will be used.

Planning Lessons Together

Once the teachers are comfortable with their room setups, we begin to look at the lessons they'll be teaching in their classrooms. I like to start our planning sessions by looking at the district expectations for a particular topic. Sometimes teachers feel overwhelmed because they are trying to teach too much. If they are focused on teaching from a textbook, they may be used to dealing with a broad range of topics sprinkled throughout the year. I ask them to consider teaching a topic in depth, over a period of weeks, thus addressing topics more deeply. I challenge them to think about this question: What is it they really want their students to understand or to be able to do at the end of this unit?

After identifying the specific objectives they want to meet, I ask teachers to brainstorm a list of materials and lessons they have available or have used in the past that address the objectives. I want them to draw on ideas with which they've had experience and that can work well with these objectives. As we go through the list of materials and lessons, I also try to suggest lessons that I think will fit in well with the topic they are teaching. In choosing these lessons, I look for mathematical lessons with the richness to address several of the objectives rather than a focus on one particular idea or skill. Lessons that use children's literature as a starting place are particularly helpful because many teachers feel more comfortable teaching language arts than math and enjoy read-alouds with their classes. Most importantly, though, I look for lessons that engage students in thinking about the mathematical ideas related to the topic at hand and in communicating about their thinking.

Modeling Through Demonstration Lessons

Teachers need reassurance that what they are trying with their students is going to pay off in terms of both understanding concepts and acquiring skills. They often benefit from seeing examples of such lessons. One way I address this need is by offering to teach a lesson at the beginning of a new unit of study. If possible, I have other teachers from the same grade level observe the class I teach, so that the whole team can begin the unit talking about a shared experience. Reluctant teachers sometimes express the feeling that while the lesson I suggest might work for me, it wouldn't work with their own students. Watching their own class with someone else teaching can give teachers a new perspective on the students through the opportunity to observe the students' reactions as learners as well as how another teacher implements a lesson.

It is important to meet with teachers both before and after a demonstration lesson. Before, I like to explain the structure of the lesson the teachers will be observing, as well as identify the important mathematical ideas I expect the students will encounter. I usually ask the teachers to focus on one thing in particular while they observe the lesson, such as:

♦ What do you notice about the questions I ask? Jot down some of the questions you hear.

♦ How are students using manipulatives to aid their learning?

♦ How do I manage time in the classroom—how much time do I spend on introduction, the group work, the final discussion?

♦ How does the room setup affect the work the students are doing?

♦ How do I redirect off-task behavior?

♦ How do I ensure that all students are participating?

After the lesson, I meet with the teachers again to debrief and talk about the question that focused their observation. I also ask them what they noticed about the students' learning and encourage them to discuss the lesson in terms of the mathematical content. We talk about classroom management, and I explain any decisions I made while

I was teaching that weren't part of the original lesson plan as we discussed it. It's important for all teachers to understand that lessons don't always go as planned, and adjustments are sometimes necessary. I also want them to understand that effective teaching calls for listening to students and moving a lesson forward based on students' reactions, questions, and comments.

Demonstrating a lesson for teachers allows me to help them see a new lesson before they might teach it. It also gives teachers a chance to deepen their understanding of what they saw by talking with me and with the grade-level team. These are some of the characteristics I look for in a good demonstration lesson:

◆ Lessons with easy preparation. Teachers can be put off by a lesson that looks like it took hours to prepare.

◆ Lessons that address more than one of our state objectives. Teachers will see that although these lessons may take a bit longer, they will help students develop in more than one area.

◆ Lessons that require students to interact with each other. This gives me the opportunity to demonstrate classroom management of cooperative group work.

◆ Lessons that call for students to share their thinking, either in writing or verbally. Having students communicate their thinking is a behavior I want to model and encourage.

◆ Lessons that are accessible to all students in the class and also of interest to those who need challenges. Later I'll discuss with teachers how they saw students engaged in different ways.

There are also alternatives to modeling all demonstration lessons myself. Sometimes I find an experienced teacher who is terrific at something that a less experienced or hesitant teacher needs to know about. I set up an observation time for the less experienced teacher, and I offer to work with that teacher's class during the observation period. This allows more observations without the cost of substitutes.

Sometimes I set up a series of classes to team teach with a reluctant teacher. For instance, if a teacher feels unsure about teaching a particular topic, we get together to plan a series of lessons that correlate to our state objectives, and then I go into the class to teach, with the teacher observing me or teaching a part of each lesson.

Final Thoughts

I try to let all reluctant teachers know that it is OK to start with small steps. Change takes time and I want teachers to see me as encouraging, rather than pressuring, them. I want them to feel free to ask questions. I also know that, for a person in my position, it is critical that I really listen to teachers. It is important that I understand what they are saying and asking.

If, for example, I am trying to engage a teacher in a discussion about effective questioning techniques and the teacher is more concerned about how to manage using pattern blocks, neither of us is likely to reach our goal. In this case, I will need to address the teacher's concerns before we are able to pursue our discussion. The more I listen, the better I am able to accomplish my own goals of helping the teachers in my school provide strong mathematics instruction for their students.

Making Sense of Arithmetic

Helping Teachers Rethink Their Practice

ERICH ZELLER

Erich Zeller works as a math and science coach at an elementary school in Los Angeles, California, with a student population of 1,200. The vast majority of the students are Hispanic (92 percent), with 6 percent Armenian and 2 percent of other ethnicities. Ninety-three percent of the students qualify for free or reduced meals, and nearly 83 percent speak English as a second language. Erich has been an elementary school teacher for the past twelve years. He was a bilingual classroom teacher for five years, teaching second- and third-grade students. He taught fourth- and fifth-grade students in an English immersion program before becoming a math and science coach.

When I first came to the school three years ago as its first math and science coach, most teachers were using a textbook as their main resource for planning and delivering mathematics in kindergarten through grade 5. Traditional algorithms were the norm: second graders learned to "carry" and "borrow," while fourth graders learned long division by dividing, multiplying, subtracting, and bringing down. Mnemonic devices for recalling rules for computation were common. While opportunities for staff development were plentiful—there were weekly hour-long staff meetings and forty-five-minute grade-level meetings—teacher buy-in and engagement were relatively low. Standardized test scores, along with a set of other indicators, including number of credentialed teachers, poor attendance, and so forth, combined to give the school an Academic Performance Index score of 1 out of a possible high score of 10.

A Focus for Change

I arrived at the school eager and determined to work toward a school-wide, meaning-centered approach to mathematics. I assumed that a clear vision for the math curriculum and how it should be delivered would ensure my easy transition from classroom teacher to coach. Now I would work with teachers to help students make sense of mathematics and be successful. I wanted to promote a shift over the next few years from a rule-bound instructional approach to one accessible to students—one that involved developing their mathematical reasoning, building on their prior knowledge, and strengthening their problem-solving skills. With this shift, I thought, students' math performance would improve because math would make sense to them and they would be confident that with enough effort they too could figure out how to solve problems. I envisioned teachers focusing on posing problems and facilitating discussions rather than giving recipes for how to manipulate numbers to arrive at answers. But communicating this big picture and how to move toward it has turned out much more difficult than I ever imagined. Looking back at the past three years, I recognize several roadblocks I encountered and false starts I made.

When I first arrived, conversations about teaching and learning mathematics, whether formal or informal, were few and far between. Also, many of the teachers, when asked, would readily admit that math was not their strong suit or that it was a low point in their day. Most seemed willing to learn more math and how to teach it. So my first effort was to engage the staff with interesting mathematical problems at each math-related staff meeting. I planned to focus on arithmetic problems, finding multiple-solution paths and communicating our strategies to each other. In fact, using and exploring alternative strategies became one of the overarching topics during these sessions and continues to be a focus for our professional development efforts.

I initially focused on arithmetic instruction because it is recognized by everyone as the cornerstone of elementary mathematics. I believed that if we could achieve a shift in emphasis with arithmetic, it would provide the leverage for examining and changing instruction in other strands of the curriculum. At the time, this arithmetic focus seemed very straightforward to me. I expected that professional development would address the many strategies that children and adults use to solve arithmetic problems and provide teachers with a menu of different problem types to engage students in problem solving. I planned to introduce Cognitively Guided Instruction (Carpenter et al. 1999) as an effective framework for this.

Making Sense of Arithmetic

I wanted to engage teachers with the idea that arithmetic makes sense when the focus is on reasoning rather than procedures. In our professional development sessions, I asked teachers to explain how they solved a particular arithmetic problem in their heads. Typically this resulted in multiple strategies, all effective for computing efficiently and accurately. For example, I asked teachers to double 27, and many where surprised at the variety of strategies reported. Some teachers lined up 27 + 27 vertically in their minds, added the 7s, carried the 1, and then added the tens. Others presented different ways of decomposing the numbers, such as thinking of 27 as 25 + 2, combining the two 25s, and adding on 4. Others added 20 + 20, then 7 + 7, and finally 40 + 14. Teachers who had not thought of these strategies saw that they were as easy and effective as using the traditional algorithm. Some teachers, searching for other ways, tried rounding up: adding 30 + 30 and subtracting 6. Still others took 3 from one 27 and added it on to the other 27 to change to problem to 30 + 24.

Alternative Strategies: A Platform for Mathematical Reasoning and Discussions

These arithmetic investigations provided the ideal background for promoting mathematical discussions. They gave me the opportunity to model questioning techniques that would get participants to analyze and evaluate each other's solutions and strategies: Will the strategy always work? Can you apply the strategy to a different set of numbers? Can you find a counterexample for which it doesn't work? These questions led to analyzing the logic behind computational strategies.

A few teachers felt empowered from these sessions to try this approach with their students. Some began to see how allowing students to choose their own solution methods led to having them decompose numbers and use place value meaningfully. Most teachers, however, resisted the suggestion of having students find multiple ways of solving arithmetic problems. Some found it perplexing, even annoying, that I was constantly asking them, no matter how simple a procedure, how they solved a particular problem. They would openly giggle when I asked, "So how did you add seven plus eight?" Even today, there are moments during conversations with me when people will endearingly add, "So, how did you figure it out?" There seemed to be a general feeling among the teachers that the math facts just need to be recalled and procedures learned. Despite all of the alternative strategies that emerged during our teacher discussions, I did not see many teachers using this approach in their classrooms. My focus on alternate strategies during professional development sessions was not yielding a noticeable impact on classroom instruction.

Teaching the Way We Were Taught

I think there are several reasons for this lack of transfer into classrooms. Teachers did not learn arithmetic this way. Because many teachers had not previously thought about alternative strategies, they questioned the validity of some of them. In some cases, this was due to a teacher's lack of content knowledge. There were instances where a child would solve a problem and arrive at a correct answer, but the teacher could not determine if the method used was mathematically sound.

One second-grade teacher showed me how a student had solved $28 + 27$ by decomposing 27 into $2 + 20 + 5$. The child first added $28 + 2 = 30$, then $30 + 20 = 50$, and finally $50 + 5 = 55$ ($28 + 2 \rightarrow 30 + 20 \rightarrow 50 + 5 \rightarrow 55$). The teacher knew the answer was correct, but wondered if this method was breaking some rule of arithmetic. My first response was always, "Well, does this always work?" Getting teachers to try the method in question with other sets of numbers tended to be helpful. We moved away from their uncertainty toward trying to figure out how a child thought about a particular solution. These experiences showed us how generating more examples and looking for counterexamples were readily available responses to these situations. Over time, many of these teachers became much more comfortable working flexibly with numbers themselves, instead of relying solely on the algorithms they had learned long ago. They began to encourage their students to think about and use different methods.

In other cases, however, skepticism toward alternative arithmetic strategies persisted. Some teachers perceived the traditional algorithms they learned as students as the "real math." Many teachers saw the practice of looking for alternative strategies to solve arithmetic problems as an idiosyncratic exercise sometimes referred to as "Erich's way of doing math," or "Zeller math." The implication was that there was the real way and there was Erich's way. In these teachers' minds, traditional algorithms were fast and efficient and the school year was already packed full of things to teach. Why would anyone spend an hour looking at different ways to add seven plus eight? It has been very difficult to make inroads with staff members who feel this way.

The perception that traditional algorithms are the real math was usually accompanied by the belief that children would be confused by these alternative ways of reasoning. At one meeting when I engaged the staff in a conversation, some teachers expressed doubt as to whether or not their students would be able to make sense of these approaches, let alone to come up with these strategies. Some upper-grade teachers thought that it was not an efficient use of time to spend a lesson looking at different ways of computing a given set of numbers. Why would anyone solve 18 × 25 by first solving 20 × 25 and then subtracting 50 (2 × 25), when they could just line up the numbers and multiply? The idea of allowing students to come up with their own procedures for solving arithmetic problems was not only new but foreign and uncomfortable to many teachers. I soon realized that belief systems would not change without concrete evidence of what students were capable of doing.

Working in the Classrooms: Evidence for Change

I decided that I needed to go into classrooms and engage students in thinking about alternative ways to solve arithmetic problems in order to produce the kind of evidence teachers needed to see when being asked to change their instructional approaches. While modeling lessons is by no means a panacea for reform-based efforts, I found that identifying teachers who were willing to begin the process of change and invite me into their classrooms brought about several significant benefits.

Collaborating with these teachers produced an initial groundswell for change that started to spread among the staff. Teachers now engaged in informal conversations throughout the day to share their frustrations, challenges, and successes. I recognized that enthusiastic teachers who shared successful math experiences during these conversations were much more likely to get a reluctant teacher's attention and trust than hours of professional development from me. In particular, teachers shared stories about how creatively students approached math problems when they were not guided to use a particular approach and when the problems were embedded in contexts that made sense to them.

I'll never forget when I heard a fifth-grade teacher share her surprise with colleagues because one of her "lowest" students had articulated a solution to a probability problem involving the most likely sum when two dice were rolled. I had introduced her students to the Horse Race problem, which involved seven horses, numbered 2 to 12—the possible sums from rolling a set of dice. To play, students rolled two dice, added the sum, and advanced the horse with that number one square toward the finish line. We asked students to predict which horse they thought would win, play the game several times, collect the data from each game about which horse won, and compare the results to their predictions.

The student who surprised the teacher most participated animatedly in the discussion. He explained that the winning horse, Number 7, won on almost all the games because there are more ways to roll 7 with two dice than any other number. After the session the teacher told me that this student rarely participated in classroom discussions, and when he did, he was usually incorrect. She admitted that when he would raise his hand, she was reluctant to call on him because most of the time he would just give a wrong answer. I asked her why she thought this time was different. She talked about several things, but what seemed most important to her was that the student had experienced playing the game himself. He was interested in the problem. This kind of evidence prompted other teachers to ask me to come in and work with their students.

Identifying a Leadership Cohort

Although not all teachers who experienced this kind of student success were ready or willing to move forward, these initial classroom collaborations allowed me to identify members of the staff who shared a common desire to change their approach or continue their own efforts at reform with the support of the math coach. I spent, and continue to spend, a good deal of my time in these "pilot" classrooms.

The positive experience of working with these teachers and their students has given me a great boost during times of doubt and frustration. I have always enjoyed working with students, and being a math coach can be very isolating. It lacks the kind of immediate feedback you get when working with students. I have come to recognize and accept that change will always meet with resistance at some level. But there are days that I feel as if no progress has been made and as if I have spent all my energy running in circles. During such times it helps to get into these classes and see the kind of math that we are working toward promoting schoolwide. This helps me keep in perspective that change is a slow and incremental process.

When I think back on what helped me identify this initial group of teachers, the leadership cohort, a few key features come to mind. While many teachers were willing to have me come into their classrooms and work with their students, this group of teachers shared some characteristics that set them apart:

- They actively engaged with their students and myself during the lessons.
- They shadowed me as I went from student to student during lessons.
- They wanted to know why I asked certain questions and not others.
- They saw students' misconceptions and confusion as opportunities for learning rather than sources of frustration.
- They were willing to implement what they saw and persevere.

One of the teachers told me that her initial decision for changing her approach was based on faith and frustration. She was not sure that this was the way to help her students, but she believed that anything would be better than trying to get her students to memorize prescribed procedures that she knew they didn't understand. She explained what happened next: "All it took was that first student solving a problem in a way that made sense to him. Soon one student grew into a few, and the few slowly became the whole class. Now all my students have access to solving problems because they have the confidence and tools to do what makes sense to them."

An Informal Protocol

To work with classroom teachers on more of a collaborative basis, I adopted an informal protocol for the demonstration lessons I taught. I gleaned this process from the many outstanding coaches and instructional leaders I have had the privilege to work with over the last three years. This process has three components: a pre-lesson meeting, an in-class lesson, and a post-lesson meeting. During the pre-lesson meeting, we identify the problems or misconceptions students are having with a particular concept. We also select what experience we will offer, make predictions about what we think will occur, and identify strategies that we want to be sure to bring to the students' attention. There are several different ways we work together during the lesson, depending on what pedagogical goals have been set. The most common is for the teacher to shadow me so that we may easily engage in conversations regarding specific decisions being made on the spot. In the post-lesson meeting, we analyze what happened and plan next steps.

A Case Study

Carmen, a second-grade teacher, met with me to plan a lesson that would engage her students with subtracting from a three-digit number that required regrouping hundreds into tens. Carmen explained that many of her students struggled with problems like these and did not apply what they had studied about place value when solving them. She saw that most of her students did not understand that regrouping from hundreds to tens involved regrouping to units of ten, not units of one. When solving $324 - 173$, for example, students using the algorithm did not realize that they were breaking up one hundred into ten tens. We decided to embed a problem in a context that would be familiar to students. Carmen would present the problem and ask students to work on it independently, either individually or in pairs. She would also encourage them, if they had time, to solve the problem in another way. Since the class was in the middle of a unit on insects, we decided to write a problem about insects flying away.

Next we focused on the numbers we would choose for the problem. I talked with Carmen about three-digit numbers that would best allow us to engage her students in a focused exploration of regrouping hundreds. I asked Carmen to consider the relationship between $320 - 170$ and $32 - 17$. She recognized that the first set of numbers had the same structure as the second but differed by a magnitude of ten. She felt that her students understood how to deal with $32 - 17$; were comfortable thinking about the 3 in 32 as thirty or three groups of ten; and could regroup one of those tens into ten units, or ones. We talked about *unitizing*, the idea that we use numbers not only for counting single units but also *groups of* ones (Fosnot and Dolk 2001). We wanted to move her students toward the understanding that the 32 in 320 could be seen as thirty-two tens.

We decided that it would be best to choose two numbers with zeros in the ones place, with no ones units to distract the children. I suggested using a problem that involved subtracting a quantity less than one hundred, to help students with the idea that, for example, sixty is equivalent to six groups of ten. We finally decided that her students would solve this problem: *Mr. Zeller had 210 insects in a cage. He let 60 insects fly away. How many insects does he have now?* We hoped that by keeping the structure of the context and numbers simple and straightforward, students would be able to solve the problem in a variety of ways that would get us talking about groups of tens and how they relate to hundreds.

Predicting Student Solution Strategies

Next we made predictions about how Carmen's students might solve the problem. We then decided on the strategies we would like to share with the class. We looked at three general solution categories: *direct modeling, counting,* and *derived facts* (Carpenter et al. 1999). Carmen knew that some of her students would solve this problem concretely, by making a set of 210 counters, removing 60, and counting what was left (*direct modeling*). The children were familiar with base ten blocks and she thought they would use them for this purpose. Carmen also thought that a few students might skip-count backward by tens (*counting*). Others, she thought, might break the numbers apart and solve the problem using *derived facts* (e.g., $60 = 50 + 10$ and $210 = 100 + 100 + 10$, so $100 - 50 = 50$, and $10 - 10 = 0$, so $100 + 50 = 150$).

Working Together

After Carmen posed the problem to the class and the students got to work, she led me to Mariana and Gretchen, who were using base ten blocks to solve the problem. The students had prior experience with the blocks and were able to build 210 using two of the hundreds tablets and a tens rod. But they were unable to solve the problem because they did not see how to take out the sixty insects that were flying away. They did not realize that they could trade a hundreds tablet for ten rods.

When we asked the girls to tell us what was happening in the problem, we realized they understood the action in the problem; they were just struggling with using the base ten blocks to represent the situation. They tried making a set of 210 *and* a set of 60, but this did not help them reach a solution. Next Mariana started drawing circles to represent the insects. When we asked her what she was planning to do, she said she was going to draw 210 circles and cross out 60. That made sense to Gretchen and they both started the tedious process. We left them to work and moved over to Alexis.

Alexis had also used base ten blocks but had successfully solved the problem. He told us that he had built 210 with two tablets and one rod, traded one of the tablets for ten rods, and removed six rods. He was now working on representing his solution on paper. Carmen and I recognized that Alexis's strategy of exchanging might help Gretchen and Mariana, so we asked him if he would share his strategy during our debriefing. He was only too happy to agree.

Next we went to see Kevin, who had several strategies that he was eager to share with us. He was most confident counting backward by tens from 210. When I asked him how he knew to stop at 150, he told me that he was using his fingers to keep track of how many tens he had counted. We asked him to demonstrate this, and he counted aloud—*200, 190, 180, 170, 160, 150*—raising a finger with each count. He stopped as he raised the sixth finger. Carmen and I spoke about how well Kevin's strategy would help students with the idea of unitizing, with each finger representing a set of tens. Kevin was more than willing to share it with the class during our debriefing.

We struggled to find a third solution that would follow naturally from the first two. Several students had used money as their model for solving the problem. They saw 210 as two dollars and ten cents. Sandy decomposed 210 the same way but subtracted sixty from one dollar to get forty cents. Then she added the other dollar to get 140 but forgot to add the dime back in. She caught her mistake after we asked her to explain her solution. We decided that if there was enough time, Sandy would share her strategy with the class. By this time most of the students had solved the problem at least one way and were beginning a second strategy or getting restless. So we asked the students to put away their materials and come to the carpet for the sharing of different strategies.

Carmen's students were familiar with the protocol for debriefing: They come to the carpet; each preselected student shares a strategy; students get to ask questions of one another; and Carmen asks students to compare and contrast the strategies that have been shared. While the students were coming to the carpet, Carmen and I discussed the sequence of students to share: Alexis, Kevin, and Sandy. After Alexis shared how he used base ten blocks, I took the opportunity to have Mariana summarize Alexis's strategy since she was one of the students who had difficulty with the idea that a hundreds tablet could be exchanged for ten rods. When we ask students to paraphrase someone else's strategy, they may begin using strategies that are new to them. Paraphrasing also keeps the audience engaged and attentive during the debriefing.

Post-lesson: Reflecting on the Experience

Carmen and I met briefly the next morning before school. During our meeting, Carmen commented on the variety of ways her students solved the problem. She recognized that some of the solutions did not explicitly involve the idea of exchanging one hundred for ten tens. We discussed the importance of being able to work flexibly with numbers and that students need to have a variety of ways for solving problems.

Most of our conversation centered on two big ideas. First, how could we help those students who did not recognize that a hundreds tablet was made up of ten tens rods? Second, how could we get students to record their thinking more accurately and efficiently? To solve these problems we looked at the need to provide the students with more math tools. The students who struggled with the idea that one hundred includes ten tens needed access to other models, such as Unifix cubes and ten-frames, that they could use to build one hundred and also to take one hundred apart again. These students had learned the naming system behind the pregrouped base ten blocks without really understanding their structure.

The second tool we discussed was the number line. More of Carmen's students needed to become proficient with unitizing sets of ten as a way of solving multidigit problems. We discussed skip-counting warm-ups using both a premade number line as well as an open number line. We would ask students to count forward or back by tens from a given number. The number line would provide an easy and effective way for communicating counting strategies. We ended by writing a new problem that Carmen would try later that week.

Moving Forward

Helping teachers change their instructional practices is never easy. And, in fact, it has actually turned out to be much more difficult than I had expected. My goal remains for teachers to teach arithmetic by drawing on students' ideas, not by presenting standard algorithms, but I had underestimated how much courage and perseverance this would require, both from me and from the teachers. No textbook spells out the scope and sequence of lessons that accomplish this task, and I underestimated the complexity of what I was asking teachers to do. The teachers in this leadership cohort have persevered through confusion and partial understandings both for themselves and their students. We are now beginning to embrace this disequilibrium as an essential part of the learning process.

I have also come to realize the importance of identifying these partners in change early on and providing them with as many supports as possible. The one-on-one work I did with their classes provided the initial momentum to pursue this approach in more depth. All of the teachers saw that they had at least one or two students who could solve a problem without being told how to do it. The teachers began to recognize and predict which strategies a given problem would elicit. They all saw the benefits of having students share their strategies with each other. They saw their students grow more confident in their abilities to solve problems. For example, Jennifer, who teaches grades 4 and 5, saw students' behavior problems decrease as her students gained access to the math curriculum. Jennifer's confidence in designing problems for her students also grew. She explained, "By listening to students talk with each other about their thinking, I was able to understand what they knew much better." This understanding in turn allowed her to meet their individual needs more effectively by writing problems that addressed the students' specific needs. This process started a positive cycle: success, confidence, effort, success.

This positive cycle has created a climate of trust—a sense of camaraderie among the teachers—and has had two major effects. First, teachers have begun observing each other teach. This has helped us all grow in our capacity to engage our students more effectively. Nearly everyone on the staff has watched one of our leadership cohort members facilitate a problem-solving session. In this way the staff can learn from the cohort's successes, challenges, and willingness to share their professional practices.

Second, Libby, a primary multiage teacher, shared an amazing by-product of our work when she described the first time her first and second graders took the California Standards Test. "I saw students confident enough to figure out problems that they had never seen before by using the tools they had constructed for themselves to solve problems."

What now? I know we will move forward by continuing to learn together—from each other and from our students. Reflecting on the past several years, I see that the process of working productively together has not been easy, and I don't expect it to become easy in the future! Targeting, analyzing, and refining instructional practices will always be challenging, but in my experience, nothing of true value is accomplished quickly or easily.

References

Carpenter, Thomas P., Elizabeth Fennema, Megan Loef Franke, Linda Levi, and Susan B. Empson. 1999. *Children's Mathematics: Cognitively Guided Instruction.* Portsmouth, NH: Heinemann.

Fosnot, Catherine Twomey, and Maarten Dolk. 2001. *Young Mathematicians at Work: Constructing Number Sense, Addition, and Subtraction.* Portsmouth, NH: Heinemann.

Learning to Look

Structuring Teachers' Observations to Improve Instruction

ROBYN SILBEY

Robyn Silbey is a veteran teacher who has worked as a school-based math specialist for more than twenty years. She works in Montgomery County, Maryland, a large, suburban school district with two hundred schools and more than ten thousand teachers. The school system is highly diversified both ethnically and economically. When Robyn created the Lesson Observation Form and the process for using it discussed in this chapter, she was teaching at a school with students from a wide variety of nationalities, backgrounds, and experiences. She is currently using the same form and process at a low-performing Title I school in the same district.

Part of my role as the school-based math specialist is to model effective practices for teachers in their own classrooms. Optimally, classroom teachers observe the lesson and incorporate some of my processes and strategies in their own daily mathematics instruction. My original implementation plan for this part of my role was to extend an invitation to teach a lesson in a classroom, teach it, briefly discuss it with the teacher afterward, and move on to the next teacher. Appointments to teach lessons were made with individual teachers during planning meetings. I met with each team, grades 1 through 5, every week during a valuable forty-five-minute common planning time that allowed us to work together to preview, understand, and make preparations for the next week's math instruction. Because I was involved in this planning, I was aware of the content taught in classrooms throughout the school. I scheduled and taught seven to ten lessons per week—about two lessons per month for each teacher.

Results using this process were mixed at best. Teachers did not necessarily focus on the strategies and methods that I so desperately wanted them to see. During the course of a lesson, teachers might ask, "May I dash down the hall to use the restroom?" "May I quickly try to reach my doctor?" "Do you mind if I grade some papers at my desk?" "Is it OK if I run to make a few copies?" and so forth. Having been a classroom teacher for more than a decade, I was sensitive to the needs and constraints of the job. So, in an effort to be a compassionate team player, I permitted teachers to grade papers, read memos, or briefly leave the room. But when I had finished teaching the lessons, I wondered what had been accomplished. Had the teachers noticed any of the effective practices I was modeling? Were any of the practices actually internalized by the teachers? Would any affect their instruction? Here is a typical exchange from that period:

ROBYN: What did you think of the lesson?
TEACHER: It was great.
ROBYN: What are some things you particularly liked about the lesson?
TEACHER: Everything.

Two years passed, and mathematics instruction at my school failed to improve. I knew that research had proven the usefulness of coaching, observing lessons, and team teaching when striving to improve instruction. I approached my principal with a new idea: a special Lesson Observation Form that teachers would use as I modeled lessons in their classrooms. The form would keep teachers actively engaged during my *modeling*. It would provide talking points during the *coaching* that followed the lesson, and it would place responsibility on teachers to *apply* what they learned after a modeled lesson. Most important, however, the form would focus teachers on best practices for *teaching* and for *learning*.

Premodeling Conference

The implementation of the Lesson Observation Form (see page 68) involves teamwork between the teacher and me two or three days prior to the modeled lesson. During a brief meeting, we review from the previous team planning meeting where my lesson falls within the instructional unit, what learning builds up to the lesson, and the anticipated prior knowledge of the students. In addition to discussing math content, we discuss teaching methodologies and techniques. Perhaps the teacher wants to see how to incorporate appropriate math terminology into a lesson or how to manage manipulatives with a large class. Sometimes the teacher asks to see how to deal with small-group instruction during a one-hour math block. Or, maybe the teacher is particularly interested in learning more about cooperative learning or classroom management techniques.

For the first modeled lesson only, we take a few moments to review a blank Lesson Observation Form. I explain to teachers that they will complete the form while watching the lesson, and that we will review the notes they take on the form after the lesson. We discuss the first two sections: *Focus on Teaching* and *Focus on Learning*. The *Focus on Teaching* section draws the teacher's attention to the four components I have found to be important for an effective lesson: the pre-assessment or warm-up; the goal-setting introduction; the lesson body; and the close/preview. This focused analysis calls attention to the unique importance of each part. For each component, I've created guiding questions to help teachers understand the intent, and teachers appreciate the detail and clarification. We discuss how the pre-assessment or warm-up links previous work to the day's lesson and builds student confidence. The goal-setting introduction clearly connects the day's learning to state or district standards. The body of the lesson is its "meat," where the teacher plans and facilitates student-centered instructional activities. The lesson closure allows

LESSON OBSERVATION FORM

Observer _____   Teacher _____   Date _____

Focus on Teaching
BRIDGE/PRE-ASSESS FOR READINESS
Upon what prior knowledge will students build for the day's learning?

GOAL-SETTING INTRODUCTION
How will students learn what they must know and be able to do?

LESSON BODY
What performance tasks, experiences, discussions, and other activities will enable students to deeply understand the essential content?

CLOSURE/PREVIEW (HOW WILL WE USE WHAT WE LEARNED TODAY IN THE FUTURE?)
What did students learn? How does it fit into the big picture? How will they build upon this knowledge in the future?

Focus on Learning
EVIDENCE OF STUDENT LEARNING
What did you observe about students' performance during an activity? Their discourse? Their written work?

EVIDENCE OF STUDENT ENGAGEMENT
How did students interact with the content? Did they work cooperatively in a group or partner setting? Did they respond to every pupil response question? Did they accept responsibility for their learning?

EVIDENCE OF DIFFERENTIATION
Were open-ended tasks, questions, experiences, performances, and/or problem formulation included in the lesson?

Next Steps
What would I like to try in my class based on the lesson?

From *The Math Coach Field Guide*, edited by Carolyn Felux and Paula Snowdy. © 2006 by Math Solutions Publications.

students to reflect on the day's work and examine it within the context of previous and future learning. The *Focus on Teaching* section addresses the teacher's presentation of material, both in terms of content and pedagogy.

This premodeling conference is essential for several reasons. It ensures that my lesson connects to the instructional unit and therefore will be appropriate for the students' learning. Moreover, it underscores the importance of having teachers actively observe during the model lesson so they can incorporate new ideas into their own effective practices.

The second half of the form focuses on student learning. Marilyn Burns says that the teacher's lament—"I taught it, but they didn't learn it"—requires a closer examination of the instructional approach. As teachers observe their students during my lesson, I want them to think about ongoing assessment, engagement, and differentiation.

First, I want teachers to specifically observe my techniques for ongoing informal assessment that gives me evidence of student learning. For example, if I pose a question for students to discuss in pairs or small groups, do their conversations indicate understanding? Are students integrating appropriate terminology in their discourse? If I ask students to demonstrate work with manipulatives, are their representations of the problem and the solution reasonable? I want teachers to recognize that as I observe students at work and I listen to their questions and responses, I am continuously assessing their understanding of the math content.

Second, I want teachers to observe their students' level of engagement. Evidence of engagement includes student behaviors such as attentiveness, rich and appropriate discourse, and staying on task. To strive for student engagement, I frequently invite students to work in small groups and pairs. I may pose a question to the class and ask each student to respond using thumbs up or thumbs down. I model for students how to "think aloud" and then ask them to think aloud through their solution strategies. I make every effort to align lessons with students' prior knowledge, both personal and academic, because teaching at the level where students are able to learn elevates student engagement. I may point out that students are most likely to be engaged when the learning is challenging to a slightly uncomfortable degree, rather than being too difficult or too easy. I also emphasize that when students are engaged, they take responsibility for their own learning.

Third, I want teachers to note how the lesson is differentiated. It is imperative for teachers to know that differentiation is *not* about duplicating different worksheets for different groups of children, but creating open-ended situations and experiences that stretch each individual student to his or her intellectual boundaries. Problem formulation, where students create their own problems following concept development, is one effective differentiation strategy. Other strategies include small-group instruction and enriching experiences that may be available and accessible to all. For example, to reinforce area as an application of multiplication, we may ask students to create a rectangle on grid paper and find its area. Students typically create a rectangle with the greatest area that they are able to compute. The activity invites each student to work to his or her maximum potential without compromising the content or the concepts.

Modeling the Lesson

Teachers have a blank copy of the Lesson Observation Form that they complete the day I model a lesson for them. They are encouraged to address all areas of the *Focus on Teaching* section and the areas of the *Focus on Learning* section that they observe. As the school-based coach, I must be mindful of each area in both sections as I plan my lesson. In other words, I have an obligation to furnish the teacher with an easily identifiable example of each part of the form during the course of my lesson. While this adds an extra pressure on me, it helps me organize myself as I plan and sets the bar where it should be for someone in my role as a teacher leader.

Postmodeling Conference

Once I've taught a lesson, the teacher and I meet as soon as possible to discuss it. I prefer to meet within twenty-four hours, because the memory of the lesson's specifics begins to fade after that time. In my many years of experience using the Lesson Observation Form, I have consistently found that teachers are delighted to be given a structured way to examine and analyze a lesson. We sit beside each other and discuss the form, working from the top of the form down. The teacher elaborates on the written comments. We may ask each other questions and discuss specific points based on these comments. If the teacher does not have any remarks written in a section, we discuss that as well. We also spend several minutes on the bottom half of the form so the teacher can share any observations of the students at work. Finally, I call attention to the final question: *What would I like to try in my class based on what I saw in this lesson?* I invite teachers to respond based on what best fits their style. Some teachers want to sharpen their math content, while others are more interested in refining their teaching techniques. Regardless of the area of growth, I find that teachers are motivated to achieve a goal that they set for themselves. With the teachers' dedication and our work as a team, the changes in teacher behavior and student learning move toward the teachers' goals.

Occasionally, teachers experience difficulty completing all sections of the form. They may become so absorbed in the lesson that they unintentionally devote less attention to the children at work. It is also possible that a teacher may have difficulty identifying ongoing assessment or differentiation. We discuss these issues, as well as any others that the teacher mentions, during the postmodeling conference.

Follow-Up

Once the modeling process is complete, I ask teachers how they would like to proceed. They usually ask me to model additional lessons. I typically model two or three lessons to provide a consistent message about the things present in virtually all lessons. Following these lessons, I prefer to move to team teaching. In this scenario, the teacher and I plan the lesson together. We each take two parts of the four-part lesson to teach or facilitate. One person teaches while the other completes the appropriate sections of the Lesson Observation Form. For example, I may do the opening and the goal-setting introduction while the teacher observes and records; then the teacher does the body and the closing while I observe and record. We both write our observations for the *Learning* section.

After the lesson, we share what we've seen for each part of the lesson. We also discuss our observations of the students. We talk about how the students responded to specific activities, approaches, or questions. Again, the teacher identifies possible areas of future growth.

In rare instances, the teacher may request to teach the entire lesson while I complete the Lesson Observation Form. Perhaps the teacher is preparing for an administrative observation or a videotaping and wants to rehearse a new effective practice, such as cooperative learning or using a new manipulative, that we have worked on together. In these instances, I'm careful to keep my observations supportive and collegial. My position as a school-based math specialist is nonevaluative, and I must be regarded as the teacher's peer and ally. My observations are designed to initiate conversations, and the teacher's responses gives those conversations direction.

Variations

I've also used the Lesson Observation Form as a starting point to initiate collegial coaching, arranging for grade-level teams to be released from classroom duties to participate in a half-day experience. The process I use for the half-day session is similar to the in-class individual modeling outlined here. First, the team and I spend about thirty minutes prior to the lesson discussing what they will see when I model a lesson in one of their classrooms. We address the items on the form by discussing (a) the lesson; (b) its goals; (c) the "look fors"; (d) evidence of student understanding; and (e) follow-up activities. Then the entire grade-level team observes me teach the lesson, and each teacher completes the Lesson Observation Form. After the lesson, we reconvene and critically review the lesson, using teachers' comments on the forms. We discuss what the students learned, how they learned it, and how the lesson could be improved. With the exception of the teacher's class in which I model the lesson, teachers use the information gleaned from the experience to teach the same lesson the next day.

The Lesson Observation Form is an integral part of my teachers' professional growth in mathematics. The form helps teachers identify and value their teaching practice as well as effective strategies for student learning. It invites the teachers to set goals for themselves, which motivates them to work diligently toward their own professional growth. In addition to the rewards of feeling better about their own instruction, our teachers have enjoyed improved student achievement in and attitude about mathematics. In short, the Lesson Observation Form focuses teachers on student learning and the instructional effective practices that optimize success.

Coteaching

A Powerful Tool

KAROLYN WILLIAMS AND CHRIS CONFER

Karolyn Williams currently teaches grades 3 and 4 in a multiage classroom at an elementary school in Tucson, Arizona. Her school has about 400 students. Nearly all receive free or reduced lunch, and many struggle with the issues that poverty presents. The majority of the students are second-language learners. During her thirteen years of teaching, she has taught children from preschool age to grade 4.

Chris Confer is the mathematics instructional coach at the same school where Karolyn teaches, in Tucson, Arizona. As part of her twenty-eight-year teaching career, Chris has supported mathematics instruction at the district level for fourteen years, has supported mathematics instruction at this elementary school along with other sites for ten years, and has been a full-time mathematics specialist at this school for three years.

Karolyn and I looked at each other in surprise. Mario was in front of the class, sharing his strategy for solving a subtraction story problem. And even though we had worked all year on strategies for making sense of subtraction, he wrote on the board:

$$\begin{array}{r} 302 \\ -\ 198 \\ \hline 296 \end{array}$$

"I can't believe it!" Karolyn whispered to me. "We've worked and worked on strategies for subtraction, and it looks like he's never seen any of them. Now what do we do?"

"Now what do we do?" That is the question Karolyn and I confront again and again in our teaching. We are both veteran teachers who have participated in extensive professional development in mathematics over the past ten years. We have attended conferences, summer math institutes, and workshops. We have listened to the foremost experts in the field, used the best curriculum in the country, and read the most up-to-date research. And still, we encounter daily situations where we are not sure of the best response.

In past years, Karolyn found that when she taught the standard algorithms, the children focused on the procedures they were expected to follow, not the meaning of the numbers. When they made mistakes, the children rarely noticed because their attention was on the steps of the algorithm, not on the numbers themselves. To address this, that year Karolyn had decided to have her students explore different strategies for solving addition, subtraction, multiplication, and division problems. She wanted to keep the children's focus on reasoning numerically and on developing a variety of tools for computing.

Over the course of the year, the students became extremely proficient using different tools such as open number lines, open arrays, and number charts. They developed efficient mental and numerical strategies based on their solid understanding of place value. However, parents and older siblings sometimes taught the traditional algorithm to the children. So the algorithm popped up from students from time to time as another way to figure. Sometimes students applied it correctly; other times they made mistakes. But what worried us most was that when students used the algorithms, they didn't understand why the procedure made sense. Their attention shifted from reasoning about the quantities to focusing on what to do with the digits. How should we deal with Mario's error, and this problem in general?

As we watched Mario, an idea hit me. "Of course!" I said. "Estimating! We need to have the students estimate before they begin, and then see if their answer is reasonable." We both knew the value of estimating, and Mario's answer reminded us why it is important.

Karolyn turned to Mario and said, "Look at your answer. Is it a reasonable answer?" She paused to let him think. "Three hundred and two is about what?"

"Three hundred," Mario answered.

"And now look at one hundred ninety-eight. What is the nearest hundred?" Karolyn continued.

"Two hundred," replied Mario. Then it dawned on him. "The answer should be around one hundred, not three hundred!" Karolyn handled the situation effectively by encouraging Mario to use estimation and focus on number sense. He erased his work, drew an open number line, and computed. "That's it," Mario announced, satisfied.

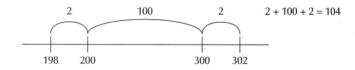

Teaching is a complex endeavor. And, through our professional relationship, both Karolyn and I have grown in our abilities to teach children mathematics. Math coaching has long been seen as a one-way street, a relationship where an "expert" provides information, demonstration lessons, and specific feedback to teachers after observing their teaching. And while these activities can benefit teachers from time to time, I find that the most powerful way that I impact the teaching of others is through coteaching and the research we do together.

As the mathematics instructional coach at an elementary school, I work with all the teachers in the building. I plan with teachers, help them find materials, help arrange their room environments, encourage them to attend workshops, help them plan and present Family Math workshops for families . . . the list goes on and on. Some teachers, however, are especially interested in changing their mathematics programs so that everything they do helps children make sense of mathematics and learn to solve problems. These teachers are in the midst of profoundly questioning what they do. It is these teachers with whom I work in a special way: coteaching.

What Is Coteaching?

Coteaching is a form of action research, where a teacher and a math coach together investigate a question related to mathematics instruction. It can be a formal investigation that emerges from a planning meeting between the teacher and myself. Or it can be a question that a teacher shares with me at incidental times such as the cafeteria line. (In line one day, Karolyn told me that the students wondered why the area formula *length times width* counted the corners twice.) It can even be a question that pops up during a lesson I am coteaching—a question that perplexes us and demands that we together use our teaching expertise to unravel the mystery of how to help all students make sense of mathematics.

Questions abound within any aspect of teaching; they hide in every corner, beneath seemingly simple exteriors. For example, the simple act of planning a lesson gives rise to questions. How should we introduce and develop mathematical vocabulary? How can we help the students recognize that this problem relates to other problems they have solved before? Will the students be more on task if they work in partners for this investigation, or will groups of four provide the students with a better repertoire of ideas and strategies?

Other questions emerge as we teach the lesson. Why did Alex arrive at an unreasonable answer? Are the students really thinking about fractions as they use fraction-strip models, or are they seeing the pieces as whole units? Why did Kasey overlap the circle units as she measured the area of her footprint? How can we support the student who showed tenuous mathematics understandings in this lesson, and how can we encourage Ricardo to extend his learning? How can we help Candice develop proportional reasoning that today was beyond her reach, and how can we help Juanita explain her thinking more clearly in writing?

Still other questions come up after school as we discuss a lesson we did that day: Where should we take the students next? What did they understand, what ideas are more fragile, and how can we continue to support students in understanding the big ideas and develop mathematical models that will help them become powerful mathematicians?

During coteaching, we present a lesson together. I may begin the lesson but hand off to Karolyn after the students understand the investigation, and Karolyn sees the point I am trying to make. Occasionally I will run into a difficulty and become unsure about how to address an idea; during these times Karolyn takes over the lesson to find a better resolution. Similarly, I take over the lesson when Karolyn runs into a dilemma. We chat together as the students work, changing our plans for the group discussion based on what we observe the students doing during the investigation.

Typically Karolyn and I will coteach several lessons on consecutive days in order to make sense of whatever we are investigating. And on any given week, I may be involved in coteaching with several different teachers. I may even coteach and research the same question with a team of teachers. The configuration changes according to teacher needs, and according to questions that naturally emerge as the year progresses.

Through the coteaching process, I learn from the teachers and they learn from me. This process is respectful of the experiences and expertise that teachers bring to professional development situations. It is honest about the fact that even very experienced math coaches cannot know everything, and that researching together is the most powerful arrangement for professional development.

What Does It Take to Coteach?

Coteaching requires a spirit of investigation and a belief that we can always improve our teaching. Rather than viewing "not knowing" as a sign of weakness, we must recognize that uncertainty is part of the process. Even expert teachers will have some questions as they research how to provide mathematical access for all students.

Both the teacher and the math coach must be able to risk uncertainty. Even though I have attended hundreds of workshops and conferences, presented to groups of teachers across the nation, and even written several books, I still have questions and always will! And exploring questions together is at the heart of coteaching.

An Example of Coteaching

At the point where the following story begins, I had focused the bulk of my instruction on the primary grades. I had long managed to avoid the big challenge faced by many intermediate teachers: how to address long division. This is the story of how Karolyn and I confronted this mystery together.

Karolyn popped into my room after school one day. "What are we going to do?" she asked, dismayed. "The children are great with multiplication strategies, and they do fine with division when they work with smaller numbers. But now the numbers they're grappling with are larger and their strategies are unwieldy. They're stuck and I'm not sure how to help!" This was Karolyn's first year teaching fourth grade. And while I was pleased that Karolyn saw us as a team that could solve problems together, I recognized the uncomfortable feeling that always accompanies a plunge into the unknown.

The next day I asked a small group of her students to come to my room. I knew that if I could better understand how a sample of fourth graders in her classroom thought about division problems, I could help find tools for us to use with her entire class. I wrote a division problem on the board:

> *Miss Karolyn had 122 pieces of candy in a tub. She wanted to put them in bags with 8 candies in each bag. How many bags of candy could she make?*

I asked the students to read the story problem and then make a picture that showed what was happening. When students sketch a problem, they often find it easier to focus on the operation. After the students shared their sketches, I asked them to estimate the answer. While several students made guesses of thirty or forty bags, other students reasoned using landmark numbers. Rebecca said, "Ten eights make eighty, so I think it's about twelve." Next I invited the students to solve the problem any way they liked.

Two students used repeated addition, adding pairs of eight to make sixteen, and then grouping sixteens to make thirty-two, and so on. Kasey repeatedly subtracted eight from the total. And the rest multiplied. For example, Julio wrote:

$$5 \times 8 = 40$$
$$5 \times 8 = 40 \qquad 40 + 40 = 80$$
$$5 \times 8 = 40 \qquad 80 + 40 = 120$$

15 bags and 2 candys left.

After school, Karolyn and I examined her students' work, and she shared with me the similar ways she had seen her students manage division with smaller numbers. Then I showed Karolyn the book *Teaching Arithmetic: Lessons for Extending Division, Grades 4–5* (Wickett and Burns 2003). We read the section "Long Division in Contexts" and thought about the alternative algorithm the authors present. We liked how the method encourages students to use their number sense as they divide, maintaining the numbers in their whole state, rather than treating each digit separately. So Karolyn and I decided to present this alternative algorithm to her students, along with Julio's method of recording. In addition, we decided that, before students did each problem, we'd have them make an estimate of a reasonable answer.

The next day we did just that. Karolyn presented the students with a problem:

> There are 584 students going to the Mariachi Conference on buses. Each bus can hold 32 students. How many buses do we need?

Before the students went to work on the problem, Karolyn had them visualize a crowd of students, standing together and then getting on buses in groups of thirty-two, and she made a quick sketch of the scenario. She then asked students to estimate what a reasonable answer might be. There were many blank looks in response to these larger numbers, so Karolyn provided some guidance.

"What if we had ten buses?" she asked. "How many students could go to on the trip?"

"Three hundred twenty," they responded.

"What if we had one hundred buses?" Karolyn continued, helping the students use what they knew about landmark numbers.

"Three thousand two hundred!" they laughed.

"So what would a reasonable estimate be?" Karolyn probed.

John had an idea. "Maybe fifteen. It's more than ten."

Anita agreed. "Like twenty or twenty-one," she said.

Karolyn looked at me, and I took over the lesson.

"How many groups of thirty-two are in five hundred eighty-four?" I asked the class, verbalizing the question that they would ask themselves. "You told Miss Karolyn that you could have ten buses with thirty-two students, and that would take care of three hundred twenty students." I wrote on the board, using Julio's representation from the previous day:

$$10 \text{ buses} \times 32 = 320 \text{ students}$$

"Can we fill another ten buses?" I asked the students. They shook their heads.

"Try two more buses," suggested Candice. So I recorded:

$$2 \text{ buses} \times 32 = 64 \text{ students}$$

"We put three hundred eighty-four students on buses," Rogelio told us. "Try two more buses."

We continued in this way, keeping track of how many students were put on buses, and in the end our recording looked like this:

10 buses × 32 = 320 students
2 buses × 32 = 64 students   *320 + 64 = 384*
2 buses × 32 = 64 students   *384 + 64 = 448*
2 buses × 32 = 64 students   *448 + 64 = 512*
2 buses × 32 = 64 students   *512 + 64 = 576*
                                 576 + 8 = 584

18 buses, 8 students left

"You need another bus for the eight kids who are left," Johan decided.

"Or send them in a van," agreed Raúl.

I then introduced the alternative algorithm that Karolyn and I had read about the previous day. "Here's another way you might record the problem using division," I explained to the students, writing the division problem on the board in the traditional frame. I extended a vertical line down the right side, explaining, "This is our thinking line."

"How many groups of thirty-two are in five hundred eighty-four?" I asked. "You told Miss Karolyn that there are at least ten." I wrote *10* on the side. "That uses up three hundred twenty students, like you said." I wrote that number beneath the original number of students, and subtracted it:

$$
\begin{array}{r|l}
32\overline{)\ 584} & 10 \\
-\ 320 & \\
\hline
264 & \\
\end{array}
$$

"Now we have two hundred sixty-four students to put on buses," I continued. "Can we use ten more buses?"

"That's too many," Laura said, shaking her head. "You could do five buses."

I continued recording as the students thought out loud, putting more students on buses and subtracting the students who still needed buses. At the end, the problem looked like this:

$$
\begin{array}{r|l}
32\overline{)\ 584} & 10 \\
-\ 320 & \\
\hline
264 & 5 \\
-\ 160 & \\
\hline
104 & 2 \\
-\ 64 & \\
\hline
40 & 1 \\
-\ 32 & \\
\hline
8 & \\
\end{array}
$$

"I get it!" said Candice, pleased. I could see from the other students' faces that this method made sense to them as well. We would certainly need to give the students more chances to use this tool, but my intuition told me that it would become very useful to them. And, in time, it did.

Reflecting on Coteaching

That afternoon, Karolyn and I discussed this way of addressing long division with the children. "I was the one looking at division from a new perspective," Karolyn admitted to me, smiling. "The children didn't even question these representations—they made sense to the children. *I* was the one feeling resistance and the struggle within, thinking that's just too confusing! But it wasn't confusing for the children. They never cease to amaze me."

Then Karolyn considered how we had worked together to come to this solution. "We solved this problem as a team," she commented. "We know a lot that we didn't know before. Next time we do this, we may change it, but we have a really good starting point." Karolyn and I discussed the adjustments we would make if we were to present this lesson again. Then we made plans for how we would continue the next day.

As for myself, I was pleased that I had acquired some new tools for teaching division, and I was looking forward to seeing how we would proceed with the unit. I had made it over another professional "hurdle." I did something that was difficult for me, and I didn't have to take the risk alone! As I thought about my good fortune to learn along with colleagues such as Karolyn, she told me, "I have really been fortunate to learn alongside you, Chris. You don't try to 'fix' me as a teacher. Instead, we coteach. You value me as a professional. We don't have all the answers yet, but we certainly are on a journey."

Coteaching Is Just the Beginning

During our investigation into long division, Karolyn and I shared our excitement and new strategies with other teachers at the school. Soon we found ourselves sharing these strategies for division with parents during a workshop. I believe this is how school change really occurs. The enthusiasm of a small group of excited teachers brings other teachers into conversations that they would never have had otherwise. As with any structure, changing one part of the system causes the rest to function differently. The small group grows, and over time the entire culture of the school changes. Coteaching is one of the most powerful tools that a math coach has.

Reference

Wickett, Maryann, and Marilyn Burns. 2003. *Teaching Arithmetic: Lessons for Extending Division, Grades 4–5.* Sausalito, CA: Math Solutions Publications.

Lesson Study

Classroom-Centered Learning for Teachers

ROSALYN HABERKERN

Rosalyn Haberkern has been involved in elementary education for thirty-four years, twenty-eight of them as a classroom teacher in a large urban district near San Francisco, California. She has also supervised student teachers and taught math methods courses in a university teacher-credential program. She currently works, part-time, as a math specialist in a K–5 school in a small, suburban district. In that position, she works with the entire range of student abilities, essentially doing whatever each classroom teacher may find most helpful.

Lesson Study is a method of curricular improvement widely employed in the Japanese education system and described in numerous articles and books such as James Stigler and James Hiebert's *The Teaching Gap* (1999) and Harold Stevenson and Stigler's *The Learning Gap* (1992). It is a process in which teachers choose lessons and set both academic and affective goals. They then refine those lessons by observing each other and meeting together to share their findings and brainstorm solutions for the weaknesses they have noted. Or, as the Japanese put it, "they polish the pearl." By focusing on how children interact with the material, teachers study the nature of learning and child development. The process can be viewed as one of peer- and self-coaching. The following is an account of my experience with one cycle of Lesson Study in an elementary school.

As a thirty-plus-year practitioner of so-called reform mathematics teaching, I have frequently been puzzled by why so little progress has been made in the United States in institutionalizing mathematics programs that develop students who are competent at and have positive attitudes toward math. Many excellent curriculums have been written, piloted, and even implemented. Enclaves of good math education do exist—from individual classrooms to schools to entire districts. However, my experiences as a teacher, math specialist, and preservice instructor in a credential program have led me to believe that most teachers are teaching math fundamentally the way they were taught. Computation may be sweetened with an occasional game, puzzle, or hands-on activity, but drill on standard algorithms remains the staple of the program. Reform curriculums often get shelved even by those who are initially receptive. Why should this be so?

The problem is, of course, multifaceted. Even with some good initial training for teachers, snags often develop when they attempt to implement a radically new approach. As this happens, teachers succumb to external and internal pressures to fall back on the tried, if not true, methods. At least, they don't have to justify and explain this different approach of teaching math to parents who don't recognize the way their children are learning long division.

My fantasy solution to this problem was that a math specialist, committed to the reform program, would be assigned to each school or group of schools to conduct ongoing professional development. This specialist would be available to respond quickly when teachers ran into glitches. I call it fantasy because of the cost of such support.

While staff development is not part of my current job description, this problem has intrigued me for years. When information on Japanese Lesson Study began to be disseminated in the United States, I thought that here might be a solution. So in 2003, when the Administrators' Conference of California Mathematics Council–North had Lesson Study as one of the themes, I prevailed on a school colleague who teaches second grade to join me in attending. I intended to learn enough to try to form a Lesson Study group at our school. Since my colleague is a person of great experience and expertise in teaching math, I knew she would be a valuable asset to the group.

It had been many years since our school engaged in systematic staff development in math. Consequently, there is little consistency in approach from grade to grade or even within a grade level. The conference I attended with my colleague increased our enthusiasm for Lesson Study as a possible way to address this inconsistency and improve overall teaching. We decided to ask the third-grade teachers to form a Lesson Study team. We chose third grade for these reasons:

1. With three classes, it was the largest grade group at our school.
2. The teachers shared similar teaching philosophies.
3. One of the teachers was a first-year teacher, and it would be a way to extend collegial support to him.

The teachers agreed to participate, and we were on our way. The Lesson Study team would consist of the three third-grade teachers, my aforementioned colleague who teaches second grade, and myself, the math specialist.

At the conference, we learned that two Lesson Study cycles per year would be a reasonable accomplishment. This seemed manageable, so we agreed to start one in October, with a second round in the spring.

Selecting the Lesson and Identifying Goals

Our first meeting was devoted to selecting a topic and setting goals. The teachers zeroed in on computation with money as an area of concern, and we considered some published materials. All three teachers were making much use of the Investigations in Number, Data, and Space materials (often referred to as *TERC*). Since we all agreed that this curriculum provides a sound foundation for students' math learning, we chose a lesson, Coupons Add Up from the *Combining and Comparing* unit, to be the basis of our project. One of our aims was for children to learn to work in a truly collaborative manner. We also wanted to increase the students' participation in post-lesson discussion.

About the Lesson

The lesson directs students to find coupons that add up to specific amounts, such as $3.70. Those teachers who had prior experience teaching the unit felt that more preliminary work was needed with smaller sums of money, and one teacher volunteered to design a lesson in which the children first worked on connecting the amount of money shown on a coupon with coins and bills. The second part of this preliminary lesson involved using coupons that added up to smaller amounts than those in the *Investigations* lesson—less than a dollar, exactly one dollar, and more than one dollar. Each teacher committed to teaching the preliminary lesson and also to making sure his or her students had the knowledge and information from the lessons in the TERC unit that preceded Coupons Add Up. We figured out when the teachers could accomplish this and then set a date for the first observation of the Coupons Add Up lesson. Our newest colleague bravely volunteered to be the first to be observed.

Following the First Teaching of the Lesson

We met a few days after our first observation for a discussion. One interesting consensus that emerged concerned the difficulties that some children had with worksheets. One item directed the students to "use only coupons for foods you would like to eat." As we circulated through the room, listening to partner dialogues, it became clear that some of the boys and girls were distracted from the mathematics by discussions of food preferences. For the next version of the lesson, we reworded the worksheet to remove the distracting words.

Another problem showed itself that caused difficulties. During the lesson, several children approached one or another of the teachers to ask if the three lines on the worksheet meant that they were to list three coupons. We learned that when a specific amount of space or a certain number of lines were provided for an answer, some students interpreted that structure as a signal telling them something quantitative about the nature of the desired answer. We reconfigured the recording sheet, removing the lines and separating the four problems on a single page into two pages of two problems.

The Second Teaching of the Lesson

Our improved version of the lesson was then taught by another of the third-grade teachers. In the meeting following this observation, we agreed that we could see that our modifications had created a better opportunity for students' conversations to focus on the mathematics. All partner interactions focused on the mathematical content of the lesson.

An additional goal, which had not been initially included in our plan, emerged from our scrutiny of the worksheet and the discussion following the second observation. Learning to read and follow directions is important for third graders, and we decided to address this in the context of the lesson. Therefore, instead of going over each problem in detail before students started, the teacher would simply make a statement alerting students to the existence of special conditions in some of the problems (to use food coupons in one and coupons for nonedible items in another) and direct them to check with their partners to be sure that they knew what to do. Then we'd ask the students to read the directions on their own.

We felt that another goal—bona fide partner collaboration—had been partially accomplished, but could use some extra attention. We discussed various ideas and came up with a possible intervention. If we noticed pairs who were not really working together, we would suggest that they alternate selecting the coupons until the goal total was reached.

In addressing the goal of increasing student participation in the post-lesson discussion, we again decided that further work was needed. After mulling over possible improvements, we arrived at some specific actions. We would ask one child to give a solution to a problem. Next everyone would indicate, in some way, his or her agreement or disagreement. Then we would ask a classmate (not the solution provider) to prove that the solution was correct—or incorrect as the case might be. We talked about taking care to set the stage for the students to see mistakes and disagreements as opportunities for learning, not as shaming or embarrassing experiences. This goal, as well as that of productive collaboration, would continue to require our attention.

The Third and Final Teaching of the Lesson

When the lesson was taught for the third time, we could all see that our work had produced a vastly better experience for our students. In addition, the Lesson Study group agreed that the experience was a very positive one. One of the teachers, our new staff member, wrote the following:

> *Lesson Study has been a powerful tool for examining and refining my teaching practice. The opportunity to observe and collaborate with other teachers is one of its many valuable aspects. If we believe that students learn best in socially interactive situations, then it seems important that when teachers engage in ongoing learning, we follow the same model. In opening our doors to colleagues, we end the isolation of the classroom teacher and place our work at the center of rational discourse.*
>
> *On the surface of this project, our group worked on developing and modifying a lesson for third graders that concerned combining and comparing numbers, using friendly numbers, and manipulating money. However, probing deeper I realized that while refining both materials and lesson procedures was an important part of our work, the residue is much greater. We engaged in reflective practice—creating thoughtful and purposeful learning and teaching objectives, using student responses to refine the lesson and assess student work, and improving our own presentations. Why is this so important to me? Most obviously, this sort of reflection is essential to continuing growth. Equally important, if we believe that children learn through their own construction of meaning, then we necessarily value process over product. As teachers engaged in Lesson Study, we, too, affirm the value of process.*

When I considered my own reactions, I realized that I had found the process to be even more productive than I had expected. As a group, we were able to uncover more problem areas in the lesson than I would have found on my own; we generated more solution possibilities. Being able to observe the lesson three times allowed each of us to think more deeply about what was happening. Because we wrote down our thoughts as we observed, we could revisit the issues and address them repeatedly, with the evidence written down before us— an impossibility for an individual working alone.

Reflections on the Experience

Unlike a more conventional form of coaching where one person's action is the subject for another's critique, no one here was the expert. Even my colleague and I, with more experience and mathematics credentials, participated as equals in the project—often facilitating but never being in charge. Since the focus was on the lesson, rather than on the teacher, everyone felt very comfortable being observed. These observations and the ensuing discussions increased the level of trust among the teachers, positively affecting the school as a whole.

Despite its glacially slow pace (two lessons per year), I believe the Lesson Study process has much to offer. In our experience, much energy was unleashed when we began to engage in this project. At the start, one teacher quickly volunteered to construct the preliminary lesson we had deemed necessary, producing exactly what was needed. Two more of us thought of extensions to challenge the more able students, though this had not been a stated goal. We were also able to think of connections to lessons that appear in other resources.

Under the day-to-day pressures of teaching many subjects and dealing with the academic and nonacademic issues that arise with a classroom of children, teachers often do not think deeply about their practice. In contrast, since four of us were able to step back from the delivery of the lesson each time, this Lesson Study experience presented the opportunity and, indeed, the obligation for just such reflection. Watching the students at work and then discussing what we observed, we were able to address such questions as:

◆ What is the mathematics in the lesson?
◆ Who isn't "getting it"? Why?
◆ How can we change this lesson to meet the needs of all students?

I am also convinced that, unlike any sort of top-down reform, this process will extend, for the teachers, beyond the single lesson studied. In time and as a result of this type of reflective practice, teachers can become their own coaches.

References

Mokros, Jan, and Susan Jo Russell. 1995. *Combining and Comparing.* Investigations in Number, Data, and Space Series. Palo Alto, CA: Dale Seymour.

Stevenson, Harold W., and James W. Stigler. 1992. *The Learning Gap.* New York: Simon and Schuster.

Stigler, James W., and James Hiebert. 1999. *The Teaching Gap.* New York: Simon and Schuster.

Helping Teachers
Take Ownership

My Goal as a Math Coach

WINIFRED FINDLEY

Winifred Findley is an elementary mathematics consultant in the Monroe, Michigan, school district. The district serves about seven thousand students in kindergarten through twelfth grade and has a poverty rate of more than 30 percent. The district has ten K–5 elementary schools, two 6–8 middle schools, and one 9–12 high school. Winifred works with all of the grades in all of the buildings, which provides for a variety of experiences and challenges.

When our district implemented a curriculum consultant program, I had been a classroom teacher for almost thirty years. I saw the consultant as a person who was welcome to share ideas with me and come into my classroom to help develop and participate in special classroom projects. Unfortunately, like several of my colleagues, I did not see the consultant as someone who might change my teaching strategies or improve my content knowledge. Many of us were content to continue doing what worked for us—or what at least we *thought* worked for us—which too often involved starting at the front of the book and going chapter by chapter as far as time allowed. While the consultant certainly passed along knowledge, the teachers did not apply it.

Our district usually took the opportunity to make any significant changes in the curriculum as part of the new textbook adoption cycle. A year after this occurred, I became a mathematics curriculum consultant. Immediately I noticed that several of the district teachers were struggling with the new materials. Many were even speaking out against it. Why, I wondered, were so many having problems understanding the new program?

As a teacher, I had often been a member of the committees making the curriculum changes and, as a result, the changes made sense to me. I even found that I was a bit impatient with some of my fellow teachers who did not like the changes. Then I realized that committee members had had an opportunity to study the research, understand the need for change, and explore the available materials. Our committee participation not only gave us the knowledge, but also the opportunity to take *ownership* of the ideas, the materials, and the curriculum itself. The teachers, especially those who were struggling, did not have that background knowledge needed to understand the changes. Therefore, they had no *ownership* in the new program's goals or approaches. The challenge for me, therefore, became twofold. First, how could I convince my fellow teachers that the new curriculum *was* appropriate and effective? Second, how could I best support the teachers to help them succeed?

Finding a Starting Place

To address this challenge, I first reflected upon what had caused me to accept change, welcome new content, try new strategies, and take personal ownership of those new ideas. From the very beginning of my teaching career, I had been very fortunate. My schools and districts encouraged me to attend workshops, try new ideas in my classroom, participate in curriculum committees, and read and share professional materials. I felt a certain amount of freedom to develop and try new teaching strategies, and to teach the curriculum the way I wanted, as long as the state and district content and expectations were met. Even so, the changes in my teaching strategies and my curriculum knowledge did not happen overnight; they evolved with experience. As well, I always had some sort of support—from fellow teachers, committee members, and, most important, my administrators.

Teachers today are pressured from many directions. They are expected to address a variety of student needs in addition to teaching the curriculum. As a result, they do not have time to keep up-to-date with curriculum changes or to try different approaches to their teaching. And yet, they feel pressured to make instant improvements in their students' progress. While I recognized that not all teachers think alike or learn or teach the same way, I decided to start with "what worked for me." My goal was to then help teachers find and perfect "what worked for them" by offering support that would allow them to grow in knowledge and understanding and enable them to be comfortable with the seemingly constant changes.

Getting Started

Although I strongly supported the district's new math program, I had only taught it for one year to fifth graders. As a district consultant I needed to get a better understanding of the content and strategies being used at other grade levels. I found several teachers at each of the other grade levels, scattered at different schools, who were willing to have me come in and get to know the curriculum at their level. Although I was there to observe and get ideas, it did not take long before I was interacting with the teachers and students, making suggestions, and even modeling different strategies.

Then something unexpected happened. As we worked together, those teachers also became more comfortable with the program and started to take more ownership of the new curriculum. Cooperation, support, and patience were making a difference. When those teachers, in turn, began to serve as the support for their fellow teachers at their buildings, it became evident to me that the teachers were taking ownership of the program. I also noted that when I would be in the buildings working with a teacher, it did not take long for other teachers to take advantage of my presence. Teachers began to stop me to ask a "quick question," which often led to opportunities where I could provide more support. Just making myself available was an important tactic. The major drawback was that although working with a teacher over a period of time on a one-to-one basis was effective, I was only reaching a limited number of teachers.

Presenting Workshops

Workshops enabled me to reach a larger number of teachers. Over the years, I have learned a great deal from workshops and have found them effective for sharing information and ideas. I set up several workshops to explain the program and share some ideas that the teachers needed to become more successful implementing it.

While there was a need for teachers to know more information about our newly adopted curriculum, it also became apparent that most teachers needed a better understanding of mathematics as well as an understanding of some alternative problem-solving strategies. Elementary school teachers tend to be better prepared to teach reading and language arts than mathematics. With less attention given to understanding mathematical concepts and more to having efficient computational skills, students often struggled with problem solving. I recognized that teachers could not truly take ownership of the content knowledge or use alternative strategies for solving problems with their students if they did not understand the math or were not comfortable with how or why the strategies worked. Therefore, a primary focus of my workshops and study groups became the improvement of the teachers' understanding of the mathematical concepts both at and beyond what may be needed at any particular elementary grade level.

However, I found it hard not to be like those teachers who try to tell or show their students not only what to learn, but how to learn it. I could hear the words "I just explained all that to you; weren't you listening?" echoing in my mind. But I remembered a favorite quote of mine, taped to the top of my planner, that comes from Marilyn Burns's book *About Teaching Mathematics: A K–8 Resource, Second Edition* (Sausalito, CA: Math Solutions Publications 2000) "You cannot talk a child into learning. You cannot tell a child to understand."

I needed to stay away from doing all the talking and telling. Teachers are not all that different from children. They, too, have a hard time just being told what to do.

To get workshop participants to take ownership of the information and ideas, I knew they would have to do more than just listen. The workshops needed to provide opportunities for group interaction and individual participation. I always tried to include at least one activity related to the workshop's focus that the teachers could take back to use in their classrooms the next day. When teachers found the activities useful, my credibility increased, and the teachers became more accepting of other ideas and suggestions.

Our workshops took on various forms. Some focused on a particular unit at one grade level; others addressed topics across the grades. Some were open to the entire district level and others were for specific schools. Some were voluntary and some were required. In schools where there were a number of teachers struggling with the program, or where teachers were not comfortable having another person involved in their classrooms, I first met with the principals to set up specific study groups or workshops that might meet several times during the year. But whatever their makeup, the workshops were valuable for providing participants with new experiences and opportunities to bounce ideas off each other. Like children, teachers learn from one another—especially when they have common experiences. Our workshop discussions led more teachers to ask me for suggestions or help with content knowledge or teaching strategies.

Moving Beyond the Workshops

We may provide teachers with all the knowledge and skills in the world, but what really matters is how they use it in the classroom behind closed doors. Improved teaching occurs not only with improved content knowledge, but with a willingness to apply what is known in a way that will be comfortable for each individual teacher. While the workshops were good for "planting seeds," the nurturing of those seeds needed to take place in the individual classrooms. It became evident to me that when I spent several days or worked through a unit in a classroom, the teacher gained a much better understanding of the content and was more willing to take the time to utilize alternative teaching strategies. Therefore, I wanted to find ways to get into the classrooms more and work with the individual teachers to provide "on the spot" knowledge and support. The frequent building visits, the workshops, and the study groups with teachers helped to lay the foundation for my credibility with the teachers, making them more comfortable with me coming in for extended periods of time.

Most often, my first visit to a teacher's classroom involved teaching an activity or game related to the area he or she was working on. This provided a nonthreatening way not only to teach or reinforce some math skills, but to establish a rapport with the teacher and the students. During discussions with the teacher before and after my visit, I included other ideas or suggestions that often led to an invitation to share another activity or even to do a lesson or two. In this way, my initial visit grew into an opportunity to nurture some of those mathematical content and strategy seeds.

Working with Individual Teachers

Spending an extended period of time with a teacher in a classroom provided me with a much greater opportunity for student and teacher observation and interaction, both purposeful and subtle. It also allowed more time for us to pinpoint growth in both student and teacher learning, and boosted the confidence levels of all.

Whether I was going in to observe, teach a game, or develop a series of lessons, I always scheduled some time with the teacher before and after the lesson. Good listening skills became an essential part of my consultant role.

During the initial meeting, we discussed what the teacher and the students were working on. We looked at some of the students' work, and considered the teacher's plans, concerns, and even complaints. That initial conversation often revealed the teacher's style of teaching, the students' levels of understanding, and the math concepts at the teacher's comfort level. We then discussed the specific goals or purposes of the games and activities. Too often these goals are not evident or get overlooked by the teacher. Finally, before I taught or modeled a lesson, the teacher and I reviewed the specific mathematics content to be addressed, the strategies to be developed, and our expectations for the students.

Just as important, if not more so, was the follow-up discussion with the teacher, regardless of the lesson or activity. These discussions took place on the phone later that day, via e-mail, or during the teacher's next planning period. Both of us needed to share how well we thought the students were able to grasp the concepts, what we thought succeeded, and what needed more attention. Follow-up discussions provided opportunities to further nurture those seeds planted earlier. They also provided opportunities for the teacher to start taking ownership of the content knowledge and strategies used.

Guidelines for Working with Teachers

My work with the teachers individually and through the workshops led me to develop some guidelines that I could use consistently with our district teachers when helping them plan lessons and also become more comfortable and more successful with teaching mathematics. I used the guidelines to help address mathematical content, to encourage the use of a variety of teaching and problem-solving strategies, to set expectations for the students, and to note if a lesson might be extended, adapted, or used for assessment purposes. While I designed them as guidelines for working with mathematics, they certainly are not limited to the teaching of math. I hoped that the key guidelines would help teachers apply what they had learned or, in other words, help them gain enough *ownership* of the concepts that they could pass that ownership on to their students.

1. What Is the Content Concept or Skill Being Addressed?

The first step to a good lesson is identifying what concept or knowledge the students will learn. This is especially important when the lesson is an investigation that expects students to construct their own ideas, or when the lesson includes a game. For example, if the students are investigating how many buses are needed to take a school on a field trip, is the teacher aware of the division concepts involved and their relationship to multiplication? Is the teacher going to address the importance of the remainder in this situation? The teacher needs to keep the content focus in mind when observing students and during discussions. That content knowledge is the foundation that enables students to take ownership for their own problem solving.

2. What Teaching Strategies Could Be Used?

It helps to focus teachers on how introducing something new is different from using lessons intended for review or reinforcement. If the concept to be taught is *new,* teachers need to pay special attention to how the concept will be introduced. Are the students going to be allowed to explore on their own? If so, for how long? What guidelines might be needed? How will the children identify and share what they discovered—in small-group discussions, whole-group sharing, written responses, or a combination of all three? What questions might the teacher ask to guide the students' discoveries and to encourage their thinking? Would teacher modeling be appropriate? If so, when? Are there other techniques or strategies that might be used to help the students grasp the concepts?

If the lesson is focusing on the reinforcement of concepts or skills already introduced, are the students expected to use alternative ways to solve a problem? How aware is the teacher of the possible strategies students might use to solve the problem and which strategies will work but are not very good or efficient? (I had a group of fifth graders present seventeen different ways to solve a homework problem one day. All of them were correct; not all of them were efficient.) Is efficiency at this point a goal? Is the teacher aware that some of the strategies students use to solve a problem are related to their level of maturity and level of understanding?

If some students have misconceptions, what might be the most effective and efficient way for both teacher and student to address those issues? Should the teacher do some modeling for a whole group and then work with a small group? Would a discussion involving all the class be effective, or some student-to-student instruction, or will individual intervention by the teacher be necessary?

3. What Are the Students Expected to Be Able to Learn and Do?

This helps to focus the first two questions. Are the students expected to solve a problem independently or in small groups? Do they need to explain how they got their answer? How will students explain their thinking? Should students be able to specifically identify the math concept or skill they are working on? Should they be able to use more than one strategy? Is the focus on being able to solve the problem or on developing accuracy and efficiency? What specific student behaviors will be addressed? Will the students be able to work well in their assigned groups and stay on task?

4. What Extensions or Adaptations Might Meet the Students' Needs?

As mentioned earlier, if students are having trouble grasping the concept or applying the skill to be learned, what other approaches might be used? Could the problems or the goals of the game be adjusted to higher or lower levels? Could the problem be modified by simply changing some numbers for additional homework practice? Is there a skill, such as some review of basic facts, that could be done for homework that would help the students be more successful in solving the problems? Does the pacing of the lesson or unit need to be adjusted to allow more time for practice or moved along to keep the students' interest?

5. How Will the Learning Be Assessed?

As the children work, what observation techniques could be used to see whether the students are learning what was intended to be learned? What written responses will indicate how well the students can apply what they have learned? What kinds of questions might give evidence of students' knowledge and understanding? Will the problem the students are trying to solve give a valid picture of what students know and are able to do? All these questions can help teachers assess whether the goal of having the students take ownership of their learning has been reached.

Summing It Up

These five key questions not only form a framework for a teacher's lesson planning and instruction, but also provide me with a valuable framework for working with teachers, both in our preplanning and follow-up discussions. As the teacher and I go over the questions, I gain insights as to the teacher's needs and concerns. I get a feel for how rigid or flexible a teacher might be and what the teacher expects from the students. I also get a feel for how comfortable a teacher is when the students come up with ways to solve a problem that the teacher may not understand.

These questions also offer opportunities for me to address any content issues and to make any suggestions. The depth in which a teacher and I may discuss any given question depends upon what the teacher particularly would like to address and how comfortable the teacher is with me. I have found when teachers talk through the guidelines with me, they are less likely to plow through a lesson without really having a vision of what they are trying to have their students do or learn.

Since many of my classroom visits include at least some modeling of a lesson, I use these same guidelines to share with the teacher when I plan. I want the teacher to know what I am doing and why. I do not like to have a teacher "sit back and enjoy the show" when I am modeling. I want the teacher to be as involved as the students. I want the teacher to be aware of the content and how it is presented, to note the strategies I am using, and to consider the student response to these strategies. I want the teacher to join me in observing the students' work and asking questions about their thinking.

My goal as a math consultant, then, is always to assist teachers in improving their classroom math instruction. Whether I work with a group or an individual teacher I try to keep the focus on their concerns and what *they* think they need. Then *I* can incorporate what I think they should know and do. If teachers are truly going to improve their teaching and understanding of mathematics, they need to take that *ownership* of the content and strategies they have been shown. Otherwise, the ideas get put on the shelf or worse, discarded. My continuing challenge is to try to help teachers be willing to understand more of the mathematics, try different approaches, and invest the time necessary to improve their students' learning.

Adopting a New Math Program

An Example of Supporting Instructional Change

MARIE BRIGHAM AND KRISTEN BERTHAO

The rural district in which Marie Brigham and Kristen Berthao work consists of two towns experiencing rapid growth. Located in Mendon and Upton, Massachusetts, the district is composed of four schools: two elementary, one middle school, and one high school, servicing approximately 2,700 students. The communities in this school district are economically diverse, but racially, culturally, and ethnically similar. No single, identifiable minority group represents more than 1 percent of enrollment. Marie Brigham has been teaching for twelve years: two years in second grade, nine years in fifth grade, and one year as a math specialist. Kristen Berthao has been teaching for eleven years: two years in second grade, one year in third grade, six years in fourth grade, and two years as a math specialist. These two teachers have enjoyed many years of collaboration dating back to their college years. They job-shared the newly created math specialist position described in this chapter for one year.

Our district's students have always performed well on standardized and state-mandated English/language arts assessments, but the math scores have reflected weaknesses. In response, the school committee became invested in bringing about positive change in the quality of math instruction delivered in the district. They charged the superintendent of schools with addressing the problem and gave him a two-year window to produce results.

To address this issue, our superintendent formed a math task force. Composed of teachers and administrators, this group identified the strengths and weaknesses of our program and instructional methods. The task force's most significant recommendations were for the district to change its math program and hire a math specialist to address the need for greater professional development at the elementary level.

Given our passion for mathematics and our interest in working part-time, we proposed that the full-time position be split so that two part-time teachers could share it. This was feasible for our district because we were each able to focus on specific grades while sharing much of the work that would affect the entire K–5 district. We were thrilled when our proposal was accepted. Each of us had more than ten years' experience teaching at the elementary level. Our passion for mathematics had driven us to engage in as much mathematics professional development as possible, and we had a long history of collaborating together. We were eager to get started!

Our first task was to create a job description. After all, this was a new position in our district. We wanted to establish clear goals that could be used to guide our work and to measure our success. In the end, we focused on areas that we thought would make the greatest impact on student learning. We decided to:

- explore reform-based math programs to be adopted for the following school year;
- model effective lessons for all teachers K–5;
- offer professional development workshops for all faculty;
- gather manipulatives and resource books to enrich math instruction; and

◆ review teachers' lesson plans, especially those of teachers working toward professional status, to help ensure that such plans met state standards.

While attention to each goal was critical to our success, this chapter focuses on the steps we took to explore and finally adopt a reform-based math program. It was important that we begin researching math programs and making plans for a pilot immediately. Our superintendent applied for a state-funded Foundation Reserve Grant in October. Monies awarded from the grant would be used to fund a new elementary math curriculum. All awarded funds needed to be spent by the end of that fiscal year (July), so we needed to move swiftly through the process of selecting a new curriculum. This was an important decision and we needed to make sure the process would enable us to select a curriculum that would best serve our students.

In November, when we knew the funds were secure, our superintendent requested that we begin researching standards-based math programs. Standards-based curriculums were the only programs considered because our success is measured by how well our students perform on a standards-based, statewide assessment. This assessment is based on NCTM's *Principles and Standards for School Mathematics* (NCTM 2000) and our state framework. After much research, three curriculums emerged as quality standards-based programs. We decided to pilot two of the three curriculums as they were widely used in our community.

The pilot was designed to involve teachers in grades K–5. Over a six-week period, piloting teachers would be responsible for teaching the one entire unit/chapter that we had selected with the publishers' consultants. The plan was designed so that two teachers at each grade level would pilot each curriculum, so we would benefit from having more than one perspective on a curriculum.

It was important to us, and ultimately to the teachers piloting, that the unit/chapter taught presented students with new material and that the unit addressed the district standards that needed to be taught at each grade level. Both publishers supplied us with all of the student texts and workbooks necessary to deliver instruction, free of charge, but our district needed to purchase any manipulative materials needed in the course of instruction. We were responsible for determining which manipulatives were needed, which we had on hand, and which would need to be purchased. Once these tasks were completed and materials were received, we planned to select and train piloting teachers.

In December, we sent an informational e-mail to all teachers explaining the pilot and inviting them to participate. We received an overwhelming response. This told us that teachers saw the need for change and they were invested in the process. As we chose teachers to participate in the pilot program, we included teachers from our Spanish Immersion program, teachers from our multiage program, and inclusion teachers, as well as regular classroom teachers. In addition, we made certain that teachers from each of our regional school district's buildings were included. In total, twenty-four teachers participated in the pilot.

Next came the task of matching up piloting teachers with a curriculum. Some of our participating teachers had previous experience with one of the curriculums or the other. In those cases, we tried to pair them up with the opposite curriculum. In this way, they would be able to share a unique perspective. Once all teachers were matched up with a curriculum, they needed to be adequately trained so that they could effectively deliver the lessons.

All piloting teachers were released from their classrooms for a half day of training by curriculum consultants from each publishing company. Training was specific to the units/chapters we were focusing on. Each consultant offered the piloting teachers contact information so that they could e-mail or phone in questions or concerns regarding the curriculum. This proved to be extremely helpful. In order to further support the teachers and familiarize ourselves with both curriculums, we also offered to model or coteach lessons with piloting teachers. Many teachers took us up on this offer.

Piloting teachers had the opportunity to visit a school in another district where the curriculum was already being used. We arranged for half-day substitutes to cover their classes. During the course of these visits, piloting teachers were able to speak with administrators and teachers involved in that particular district about the selection and implementation of their new standards-based curriculum. Our piloting teachers were curious about how the curriculum was adopted. They wanted to know if the district had phased in the curriculum or adopted it all in one year. Piloting teachers were also very concerned with training and asked how much training the teachers had received prior to the adoption.

After these meetings, piloting teachers were invited into a class-room to observe a lesson. Experiencing actual lessons enabled piloting teachers to see clearly the difference between these curriculums and the program we were currently using. Piloting teachers were impressed with the seamless integration of manipulatives and the apparent high level of student understanding. After these site visits the piloting teachers were hungry for change.

Midway through the six-week pilot period the curriculum con-sultants from the publishing companies came back to meet with pilot-ing teachers. Substitute teachers were again secured to cover piloting teachers' classrooms while they met with the consultant and us. Both of the curriculums being piloted were drastically different from our current curriculum. Our students had become accustomed to a pro-cedures-based curriculum that demanded little deep thinking on their part. Because of the vast difference, some teachers were frustrated and overwhelmed by their pilot curriculum. This opportunity to meet with the consultant let them air their concerns. During these meet-ings, teachers asked questions, shared concerns, evaluated student work samples with the consultant, and discussed any necessary changes.

At the end of the six-week piloting period we presented teachers with the following questions to consider in the form of a survey:

1. Was the unit you piloted engaging for all students? Do you think the students enjoyed math more?
2. Did the unit prepare the students to meet state and district standards? Please provide an example.
3. Did the unit provide for the differentiation of instruction? How?
4. How did your special education students progress during the unit?
5. Was the unit teacher-friendly? Please give an example.

6. What are some strengths of this unit?
7. What are some weaknesses of this unit?
8. Did the unit allow students to construct knowledge using problem-solving and thinking skills? Please give an example.

Once teachers had an opportunity to think about and respond to these questions we invited them to meet with the superintendent, the director of curriculum, district principals, and parent representatives. Teachers brought their completed surveys and any student work samples they wished to share. We set up two separate meetings—one for each curriculum. In this way, teachers didn't need to feel like they were competing with each other to "sell" their curriculum. Both groups of teachers truly loved and felt passionate about the curriculum they had piloted. They clearly stated that the pilot standards-based programs allowed their students greater access to high-level mathematical concepts. Piloting teachers were surprised at the deep level of understanding their students had displayed.

We had determined that the administrators would listen to feedback from both groups of piloting teachers and then make the decision to go with one program over the other based on this feedback. We wanted to avoid having the decision come down to a teacher vote, which would mean that some teachers would "lose." We didn't want teachers to feel as though the district was adopting a program that they hadn't supported. In the end, we knew that our administrators would rely on the teachers to help them make a well-informed decision with our students' best interests in mind. After both meetings were held, our administrators were thrilled with the feedback they had received on each curriculum. It seemed as though we couldn't go wrong with either one.

Shortly after both meetings, our administrators made the decision. All piloting teachers were invited to attend a brief celebratory meeting where an official announcement regarding this important curriculum decision would be made. At the meeting, our curriculum director thanked all piloting teachers for their time, extra effort, and valuable feedback. He also stated the main reasons that led our district administrators to choose one program over the other. Finally, we wrote a letter to the entire school community that announced the new curriculum and outlined the decision-making process. We explained the reasons why we selected that particular curriculum:

◆ The exploratory nature of the lessons allows students to construct their own knowledge of mathematics. This will allow our students to understand mathematics at a conceptual level.

◆ Teacher professional development is embedded in the curriculum, which will help our teachers to increase their own knowledge of the math they teach.

◆ The lessons are well developed, which will allow teachers to deliver instruction with confidence during the implementation years. Lessons are laid out in a vignette style so that teachers can envision what will unfold in their classrooms before they even teach a particular lesson.

◆ The consultants offer impressive support and professional development. They were extremely attentive and helpful during the pilot process, and they have a reputation for excellence in districts where the curriculum has already been implemented.

◆ This math program can be phased in gradually during the implementation years because the curriculum is organized into separate curriculum units. A more gradual implementation will make this instructional shift less stressful for our teachers and students.

For the first time, teachers would not have to hunt for lessons and scramble for manipulatives. They would have a cohesive curriculum complete with all the tools necessary to deliver a first-class mathematics education.

Our next goal was to have the new curriculum in the hands of teachers before the end of the school year. This would allow teachers to review the curriculum over the summer and make summer plans for professional development. While we were thrilled that the selected curriculum had professional development embedded in it, we knew that additional rigorous professional development would be needed.

Tackling the task of offering essential professional development became our next focus, but that is a tale for another time.

The truth of the matter is that we did not finish our job in one year. There is still much work to be done. With a new standards-based reform math program in place, professional development will always need to be ongoing. The nature of math instruction has changed. Our teachers will need to continue to focus on developing their own understanding of the math they teach as their methods for delivering the instruction continue to improve. Providing meaningful professional development is a necessity, especially during the first year of implementation. Modeling and coteaching will also be a primary focus of the math specialist. Seeing the math come alive in the classroom will always be the most exciting part of this job. Knowing that we've made a connection with the teachers we serve helps us feel optimistic about the direction our work will take in the future.

Reference

NCTM. 2000. *Principles and Standards for School Mathematics.* Reston, VA: NCTM.

From the Trenches

Lessons Learned

PATRICIA E. SMITH

Patty Smith has been a math educator in South Carolina public schools for more than thirty-five years, as a teacher, a district math supervisor, a school-based math specialist, administrator, and grant writer. Most recently, she has been a K–8 math consultant in numerous schools and districts in South Carolina, Ohio, Indiana, Illinois, and North Dakota. As the coordinator of a large National Science Foundation Teacher Enhancement grant, she spearheaded the extensive math professional development of teachers, teacher leaders, and math specialists in fifteen elementary schools in her district. Since 2001, she has been coaching and mentoring teachers in low-achieving elementary and middle schools.

In September 1990, I temporarily left my position as a district math supervisor to forge new ground for one year as a school-based math specialist. My purpose was to promote professional growth and change among teachers. This effort was funded through a state innovative school grant I had written for Allison Elementary School. Just two months into this new and challenging role, I learned that I had received the 1991–1992 Christa McAuliffe Fellowship for my state, which would enable me to continue developing a math-specialist model for school-based change. Away from school the day I received the news, I excitedly called the principal: "Tell everyone I will be back for another year!" She responded, "Maybe we should wait until you return to school and we'll talk about it." Not all of the teachers were excited about the prospect of having me around for another year!

Lesson 1: Change Teachers' Perceptions to Change Their Reality

When we recognize teachers' experiences and perceptions, we can begin to plan the best way to move the school forward. Thankfully, my principal had the courage and foresight to share with me the teachers' concerns and perceptions that I, in my zealous quest as a math missionary, had failed to recognize. She reminded me, first of all, that the teachers taught *all* subjects—so they weren't nearly as enthusiastic as I was about the new NCTM Standards and changing what they taught and how they taught it. She emphasized that teachers' planning times were sacred, so during my weekly meetings, I needed to be on time, have a planned agenda, and provide them with lessons and resources that were interesting, useful, and relevant to both their immediate and long-term needs.

Since I had already served as a district math leader for thirteen years, I had a head start on understanding the evolution in math content and the direction in which NCTM was leading teachers and schools in changing curriculum, instruction, and assessment. However, these reforms were new to most of the teachers. In spite of my eagerness to accelerate school and teacher reform at a rapid rate, I learned that I would have to work with the teachers at their own level and pace, slow down, and nurture and mentor each teacher individually as we traveled the road to reform together.

My one year turned into almost three years at Allison Elementary, including teaching all subjects during a six-month return to the classroom as a self-contained fifth-grade teacher with a heterogeneous class. This last experience regrounded me in all the realities that classroom teachers face and proved to be the most valuable of my experiences at Allison Elementary.

During those years, exciting, dramatic, and meaningful changes unfolded at Allison. The school became a nationally recognized model for NCTM Standards reform. Use of manipulatives increased dramatically and textbook dependence decreased. All of the teachers became leaders in their own area of interest. Some developed math topics; others wrote and implemented thematic units. Some became experts in specific hands-on instructional strategies; others learned to teach problem solving quite effectively. We initiated several schoolwide math activities that energized not only the teachers but also the students, parents, and local community. These included Math Moms, a group of parents who received training to support classroom instruction; a series of Family Math Nights, which were led by various faculty members and administrators; a Superstars problem-solving program, which was maintained by parent volunteers; and a construction math project, which coincided with the building and remodeling of the school and connected math to practical applications such as plumbing, structure, electrical, carpeting, and landscape. The teachers began to see themselves as leaders, sharing and demonstrating their new areas of expertise with each other and with visiting teachers from other schools and districts. Many wrote and received teacher grants to explore their creative, standards-based ideas. Two even went on to become the state recipients of the Presidential Award for Excellence in Elementary Mathematics!

Lesson 2: Change the Culture from Within, Rather than from the Outside

During a period of seven years I served as a school-based specialist at a total of four schools, including Allison. My aim was to promote change where it matters most: within classrooms, within teachers, and ultimately, in student learning. Because my time in each of the four schools was limited (one or two years per school), I had to quickly assimilate myself into the school culture—defining and understanding the "territory" early on. Understanding the perspectives and expectations of major stakeholders is essential, so initial conversations with teachers, administrators, a sampling of parents, and even students are important. Understanding school politics is also critical. Who really has the power? The authority? The commitment? Who will share our vision and support our efforts?

Frequent meetings with teachers are essential, but they have the greatest impact when they are filled with useful ideas and helpful resources that address the needs and interests previously communicated by the teachers. Lest teachers perceive a specialist as another initiative from the outside that will soon go away, it is critical to promote change from the inside, by understanding where teachers are coming from, what they face on a daily basis, what their interests and apprehensions are, and what resources (or lack of) they have available. Yes, we specialists do have an agenda—but we can best accomplish it by assimilating our vision into the school culture.

At Bent Creek Elementary, my second school, teachers were interested in connecting math across the curriculum and to the real world. We spearheaded the 100th Day celebration, developed Pumpkin Math lessons for every grade level, and implemented numerous grants, such as Food Math, Grandma Math, Real Estate Math, and Math in Careers. At Cants Corner Elementary, my third school, we focused on raising math awareness among teachers, students, and parents. We developed a model for staging a Math Fair competition and held a schoolwide Math Door contest. At Dover Park Elementary, my fourth school, the high concentration of at-risk students created the need for models for professional careers, and our families needed exposure to better health habits and information. So we wrote and received a Toyota TIME grant to collaborate with the nearby hospital to develop a yearlong math and medicine curriculum for the fifth grade. The four fifth-grade teachers learned about collaboration and division of labor, each assuming a unique leadership role in order to successfully implement this complex project.

When math specialists assimilate into the environment and understand its culture and social systems, it is possible to establish a realistic vision of what can be accomplished within the given time frame. Written goals and a time line, both modified as needed, can help us stay on track. We must consider how the culture will look in one year, two years, five years. How will teachers change? How will classroom instruction change? What are realistic student performance expectations? It is best to share this vision with the principal or curriculum coordinator to be sure there are no major conflicts. Then we can move forward, always staying true to our vision.

Lesson 3: Recognize That Teacher Empowerment and Collaborative Leadership Will Promote Longer-Lasting and Deeper Change than the Work of a Short-Term, Single Leader

Through every project and endeavor I witnessed, new teacher leadership and expertise emerged, and collaboration and collegiality in each school grew stronger as shared goals were attained. There are no guarantees that a specialist will stay in a school very long. It's nice to take credit for changes that occur, but the true test is if those changes last and if growth and leadership continue when the initial support departs. Therefore, it is essential to develop the unique strengths and interests of each teacher, so that, collaboratively, the school can continue down the evolving road of math reform.

Even with the greatest depth of knowledge, training, and expertise, a specialist can't possibly be an expert in every grade, topic, and resource. A smart teacher leader will nurture and acknowledge the development of expertise in every teacher, then find ways for that expertise to be shared. This can be done through informal share sessions, by asking teachers to lead inservices, and by enlisting teachers to speak at conferences. Most first-time speakers need delicate support and hand-holding to get them through their first speaking experience, which can be somewhat intimidating and challenging. However, when teachers see the appreciation of the audience and the respect for what they have to share, these new presenters are often hooked and willing to do it again!

One year I asked the specialists and lead teachers in my NSF project to plan several original Math Outside the Walls sessions for our state math conference. Working collaboratively, they traveled to Myrtle Beach, South Carolina, and visited malls, supermarkets, stores, an amusement park, the convention center, the food court, the cemetery, and a minigolf course to develop thematic lessons and problems that connected to real-life applications. This activity elevated these teacher leaders from school-level to state-level leadership roles. Some even went on to present at NCTM regional and national conferences.

Another effective technique for cultivating emerging expertise and leadership is to release teachers to observe the classes of other "expert" teachers or to meet with these experts during planning times. When teachers create successful lessons, thematic units, and other projects, specialists can ask them to write up brief summaries to share with their peers. Many teachers don't believe they have anything of merit to share with others, although they are often eager to receive others' resources and ideas. Through gentle nudging a math specialist can give teachers validation along with a "license to share." Fostering sharing opportunities will help form a more collegial, give-and-take environment within the school where teachers help each other grow professionally.

One of my favorite methods of nurturing professional growth is through writing and implementing grants. Any teacher with a creative or an innovative idea is capable of learning to write a grant. Once funded, teachers develop tremendous confidence, self-esteem, and a new sense of worth as they implement their grants. Early in my career as a district supervisor, one of my bosses told me that "money is power." Through grants, teachers become empowered to change and improve their classroom instruction and student learning in the ways they decide are most appropriate. Receiving grant funding reaffirms for teachers that their ideas are meritorious. My favorite funding sources include NCTM and state math organizations, state and district grant programs, Toshiba, NEA, Michael Jordan Fundamentals, and Unsung Heroes (ING). Professional organizations, state departments of education, and local districts also provide valuable leads to funding sources. District grant writers often provide helpful hints for writing grants on their Web sites, as do many of the funding organizations.

All of these types of activities help to whittle away many teachers' self-perceived myth that they don't have anything valuable to contribute to the profession outside their classrooms. By engaging in these activities, teachers establish a credible niche for themselves in the leadership scheme. If their contributions and efforts to learn and lead are regularly recognized and appreciated, they will continue to blossom. The whole school benefits from each new accomplishment.

Lesson 4: Form an Agenda Based on Teachers' Natures, Needs, and Interests

The long-range goal of most specialists is to improve the depth of teacher knowledge and the quality of instruction and, ultimately, student learning. Specialists can stay focused on this goal by viewing themselves as an extension of the teachers. A specialist enables and encourages teacher growth by providing opportunities for them to learn, improve, and be innovative. These opportunities must reflect the natures of the teachers themselves. Even teachers who teach the same grade have different personalities, teaching styles, learning styles, knowledge bases, experience, training, attitudes, and dispositions. It is unproductive to treat all teachers the same or expect the same responses from everyone. Every teacher has strengths and interests that math specialists can build on. The challenge is to discover and uncover them. Every teacher's unique contribution is important to building a strong, collaborative leadership.

Math specialists must take the time to get to know each teacher—asking questions, listening carefully, and observing teachers as they interact with others and with their students. Instead of becoming the teachers' new best friend or confidante, we must strive to become their best professional friend: their mentor, their supporter, and possibly even their role model. I can't stress enough the idea of active and frequent listening, using what teachers say to steer our course and help us understand the teachers' needs. Even their casual comments can prompt us to entice them to try a new idea, reconsider a belief, or seek out new information. Support comes in many forms, so the type of support we give each teacher must also match each individual with whom we work.

Lesson 5: Model and Promote an Attitude of Lifelong, Collaborative Learning

Many teachers practice in an isolated environment, with little opportunity to interact with and learn from adult peers. Most of their adult learning is formal, accomplished through graduate coursework, inservice, and reading. However, with a school-based specialist on board, effective learning for teachers can also take place in their own classrooms and school, and from their peers and teacher leaders. Specialists can open the door to many new opportunities by asking teachers to share, present, teach their peers, conduct action research, develop written lessons and units, and implement grants. The specialist provides ongoing scaffolding and support as teachers embark on these new learning ventures.

As a mentor, a specialist must be able to share knowledge, experience, and expertise, and respond to teachers' interests, needs, and requests. We must take time to gather and learn new information, and to share what we already have and know. It is best to capitalize on our current strengths while working on our weaknesses. Requests by teachers for lessons and resources outside of our comfort zone may seem intimidating, but a little time and courage, along with the right resources—including other teacher leaders and teachers with specific expertise—will enable us to provide what our teachers need.

Accessibility to high-quality professional resources is essential for a math specialist to function efficiently and effectively. Useful, standards-related information is readily available through organizations such as NCTM and NCSM in the form of publications, e-resources, conferences, academies, and peer interaction. Like it or not, a specialist is perceived as an expert. These are big shoes to fill, but it's all right to admit we don't know something, as long as we promise to try to find out.

A specialist never stops learning in this position. Since time is always of the essence, it is important to organize new information so we can readily find it later. My teachers used to remark that my office was organized chaos; yet I could always get my hands on an article, lesson plan, or manipulative quickly. If it takes too long, the opportunity to make a difference is gone. The teacher moves on to a new topic and won't need the information till next year!

A specialist who is willing to model lessons with real students gains tremendous credibility and respect from teachers and sets an example of taking risks, exploring new territory, and learning by doing. It also sets the stage for trust and collaboration, especially if the teacher has struggled with that particular concept or skill. Every demonstration lesson doesn't have to be a showcase lesson. We must take heed, how-ever, to set some ground rules for demonstration lessons:

1. The teacher remains in the classroom and does not use this as a free time to take a break.

2. The teacher actively participates and does not sit at the desk grading papers or simply observing.

3. Both specialist and teacher are there to learn from the experience and will discuss and reflect on the lesson afterward and even dur-ing the lesson.

Specialists should encourage teachers to sit by students and note students' responses, how they follow directions, and what thinking processes they follow. Teachers should also move around the room observing and asking questions. It's also a good idea for at least one other teacher to observe the lesson; two perspectives and memories of the les-son are always better than one, and this provides another opportunity for teachers to reflect, communicate, and collaborate with each other.

Teaching demonstration lessons is a powerful way for specialists to build a repertoire of instructional strategies as well as content knowl-edge. A short written lesson plan will encourage future replication in other classes, and it will free teachers from taking notes during the demonstration, allowing them to participate more actively in the live lesson. I developed a simple form that I filled in for each new lesson (see page 119).

With all the wonderful resources available, it is often unnecessary to create an original lesson, but rather to cite and summarize a pre-existing lesson from sources such as the three Collection of Math Lessons books, the six Math By All Means books, and Marilyn Burns's *About Teaching Mathematics, Second Edition,* all from Math Solutions Publications. I also rely on the Standards-based Navigating series pub-lished by NCTM. Over the years I have amassed hundreds of lesson plans that I have both used and shared with many teachers.

Specialists working with multiple grade levels will want to build an extensive collection of teacher-friendly resources. In order for teachers

MATH LESSON

TITLE: _____

GRADE LEVEL(S): _____ TEACHER: _____ DATE: _____

LESSON SUMMARY:

TOPICS/THEMES:

STATE CONTENT STANDARDS:

NCTM PROCESS STANDARDS:

_____ Problem Solving   _____ Connections   _____ Communication
_____ Mathematical Reasoning   _____ Mathematical Representation

MATERIALS:

RESOURCES/REFERENCES:

LESSON NOTES/MAJOR INSTRUCTIONAL STEPS:

ASSESSMENT IDEAS:

to learn in a way that changes their thinking and teaching, they must have access to current resources that support the NCTM Standards in mathematics content, instructional strategies, and assessment. The specialist is the clearinghouse for these resources. Networking with other specialists and teacher leaders is most helpful for both sharing and acquiring ideas. Attending conferences enables us to gather ideas and handouts to share with teachers and to interact with experts from numerous venues (classroom, university, consultants). Most speakers now provide an e-mail address and are very helpful when contacted online. Specialists should make time to peruse the exhibits at conferences, carefully evaluating the products to determine which ones will best support the standards and the needs of the school and teachers. Of course, the available bounty of Web sites offers endless resource possibilities, but we must be sure to screen them carefully. Quality of resources is extremely important. Shallow, cutesy, irrelevant, non-standards-based, outdated—these are just a few characteristics of resources that could do more harm than good and destroy our credibility as professionals, so we must be careful of what we share in an effort to provide information to our teachers.

Lesson 6: Model and Promote Professionalism

Specialists need to make every minute count. Change takes time, effort, and perseverance—and we may not have forever to bring about measurable change in our teachers' instruction and students' learning. We should always have a plan, but know that it is subject to change. We must give adequate time to all groups and balance our services (such as demonstration lessons, mini-workshops, special projects, meetings with individual teachers, research, and planning). In most schools, specialists receive little to no direction for planning their schedules, so it is important to take the initiative in setting priorities.

Persistence is important. Specialists should stay in contact with *all* teachers, even those who seldom respond to our offers for assistance. We can never know when the reluctant teacher will voice an interest or drop a hint of need—we must be ready to spring into action and capitalize on the moment. Oftentimes I would send a written message to all teachers but not receive a response from some. Rather than assume they were not interested, I would contact them again, and even again. Sometimes I would call them or check with them in person. With all that teachers have to do, ignoring a specialist is usually not intentional, but establishing contact often moves to the bottom of their priorities.

To give teachers a sense that I was truly there for them and took my job as a change agent seriously, I distributed a weekly calendar that noted every teacher I planned to work with, including the day, time, and nature of the activity. I noted time not spent in classrooms or meeting with teachers with phrases such as *work on grant, organize materials, plan lessons, analyze test scores, plan workshop.*

Staying on time is another challenge, because it's easy to get tied up in a classroom or be flagged down in the hall by a teacher with a question or request. It is especially critical for specialists to be on time for meetings during planning times and for scheduled demonstration lessons. A few tardies will seriously damage our credibility and send a message to teachers that their time is not as important as ours.

Dependability is an essential attribute that builds trust and collegiality. Specialists should make a reminder note when teachers ask for a resource or for help. It's also important to respond to e-mails in a timely fashion and to schedule teachers on a calendar. If neglected or forgotten a few times, many teachers will just not bother to approach a specialist again. Our success depends on our relationship with the teachers, so they must be able to count on us.

In some of my schools, a duty was required, such as car duty, lunch duty, or playground duty. Even when it was not required, I still volunteered for a duty to show teachers that my time was no more or less valuable than theirs. As much as I loathed the duties, they helped me to be a part of the culture, not apart from it. I viewed each duty as an opportunity to bond with someone, usually the teacher I had duty with. Specialists, when given a choice, should ask for a duty that will allow them to serve with (and hopefully connect with) a variety of staff members.

Specialists must also refrain from gossip—which is difficult in some school settings. It is essential to be very careful not to reveal personal and professional tidbits teachers have shared or behaviors that have been observed. Breach of trust will seriously undermine everything we are working to build with our teachers. Gossip and chat also take valuable time away from the job we are there to do.

Lesson 7: Practice the "Water Principle"

Specialists should go with the flow and start with the area of least resistance. We will always have more to do than time to do it, so it's best to start with those most willing to buy into reform. Peer success and interest will help get others on board, and some teachers will relate to their peers (with their newly developed expertise and enthusiasm) more than to specialists.

Learning to use manipulatives is a good case in point. We all know that placing large quantities of manipulatives in classrooms doesn't ensure that teachers will use them. However, when teachers actually see how manipulatives can be effectively used, they are more apt to incorporate them into their instruction. To engage all teachers in using manipulatives, specialists can start with those classroom teachers who are willing to learn how to use a particular manipulative effectively to teach a specific skill or concept. Specialists can then model its use in the interested teachers' classrooms, sharing lesson plans and resources to further support the teachers' experimentation with the materials. This creates more leaders with specific areas of expertise. Teachers with similar needs can then invite the "expert" teachers to step in and provide the demonstration, explanation, and mentoring needed to use the manipulative.

Specialists can also create "teacher need" by modeling the use of a particular manipulative to teach a challenging skill. Once teachers observe how the manipulative helps their students understand the skill or concept, they may request the materials for their own use.

Lesson 8: Strive to Be an Effective Leader

Most teachers don't formally learn how to lead adults, so when we assume the role of school-based specialist we must reflect on the type of leader we are and need to be for our situation. Most specialists are not administrators and have little direct access to funds (which is why grants are so helpful). We are not tied directly to teacher evaluation, which is better if we are truly trying to change the beliefs and practices of teachers. Therefore, it is necessary to develop and utilize leadership skills that enable us to accomplish meaningful and lasting changes within our schools in a subtle, behind-the-scenes way. There are countless books and articles on leadership to guide us on our journeys. Those that address leadership in the school setting are especially helpful. In *The Leadership Challenge* (2002), James Kouzes and Barry Posner provide a simple guide by identifying five practices of exemplary leaders: Challenging the Process, Inspiring a Shared Vision, Enabling Others to Act, Modeling the Way, and Encouraging the Heart. For new teacher leaders right out of the classroom, just a few good books can help set the stage for the challenging journey ahead. Two very informative books are *Teachers as Leaders: Evolving Roles* (Livingston 1992) and *Building a Professional Culture in Schools* (Lieberman 1988). Both are collections of articles by experienced teacher leaders, professional development providers, and researchers in the field of school-based leadership and culture.

At this point my public education career has spanned thirty-seven years—as teacher, district math coordinator, school-based specialist, school administrator, grant writer, and consultant. My seven years as a school-based math specialist, however, were by far the most rewarding, professionally stimulating, and satisfying years of my career. In this position we can make and witness change on a daily basis. We can enable new and energetic young teachers to take wings and soar. We can rekindle the fires in burned-out teachers. As important change agents, we really can make things happen!

References

Caffarella, Rosemary S. 2002. *Planning Programs for Adult Learners: A Practical Guide for Educators, Trainers, and Staff Developers.* San Francisco, CA: Jossey-Bass.

Glatthorn, Allan A., and Linda E. Fox. 1996. *Quality Teaching Through Professional Development.* Thousand Oaks, CA: Corwin.

Kouzes, James M., and Barry Z. Posner. 2002. *The Leadership Challenge: How to Keep Getting Extraordinary Things Done in Organizations.* San Francisco, CA: Jossey-Bass.

Levine, Sarah L. 1988. *Promoting Adult Growth in Schools: The Promise of Professional Development.* Boston, MA: Allyn & Bacon.

Lieberman, Ann, ed. 1988. *Building a Professional Culture in Schools.* New York: Teachers College Press.

Livingston, Carol, ed. 1992. *Teachers as Leaders: Evolving Roles.* Washington, DC: National Education Association.